Starting Drama Teaching

Second Edition

Mike Fleming

 David Fulton Publishers

This edition reprinted 2009 by Routledge
2 Park Square, Milton Park, Abingdon, Oxon OX14 4RN
Simultaneously published in the USA and Canada by Routledge
270 Madison Avenue, New York, NY 10016

First published in Great Britain in 1994 by David Fulton Publishers
Second edition published 2003
Transferred to digital printing

Copyright © Michael Fleming 2003

Note: The right of Michael Fleming to be identified as the author of this work has been asserted by him in accordance with the Copyright, Designs and Patents Act 1988.

British Library Cataloguing in Publication Data
A catalogue record for this book is available from the British Library.

ISBN 1 85346 788 X

All rights reserved. No part of this publication may be reproduced, stored in a retrieval system or transmitted, in any form or by any means, electronic, mechanical, photocopying, or otherwise, without the prior permission of the publishers.

Typset by Pantek Arts Ltd, Maidstone, Kent

Contents

Acknowledgements

I am grateful to my wife Marianne who gave many suggestions which improved the content and style of the text and whose support has been inestimable.

Acknowledgement is made to Faber and Faber Ltd for permission to reproduce 'My Parents' from *Collected Poems 1928–1985* by Stephen Spender; to Mrs A. M. Walsh for 'The Bully Asleep' by John Walsh from *Poets in Hand* (Puffin Books); and to David Higham Associates for permission to reproduce 'What Has Happened to Lulu?' by Charles Causley.

In one corner of an infant classroom a small group of pupils is busy playing. One is pretending to be a doctor, another a nurse and two are patients. One of the patients is being 'bandaged' and the other is having his temperature taken. In the secondary school nearby a drama class is taking place with a group of eleven-year-olds. Their drama is based on the story of the Pied Piper and in pairs the pupils are improvising a very simple scene in which two neighbours have mixed feelings of embarrassment and relief when they discover that both have an infestation of rats. Elsewhere in a theatre a group of professional actors is in the final stages of rehearsing a scene from *King Lear*.

Each of these activities could come under the umbrella concept of 'drama' used in its broadest sense. However, if we wanted to divide the activities in some way, which two have more in common? Which two activities have a 'family resemblance' and which is the odd one out? Of course there is no correct answer because it depends on what criteria we invoke. It would not be wrong to say that the first two have more in common because they take place in schools, although that would be a fairly superficial categorisation. Another approach is to argue that the first and second cases are examples of 'drama' (seen as creative, self-expression) and the work on *King Lear* is an example of 'theatre' (involving acting and performing). Or it is possible to say that the first two belong together because the pupils are not working from script. However, there is a less obvious but compelling case to be made for grouping the Pied Piper and the *King Lear* examples as instances of 'drama as an art form' (involving the conscious crafting of meaning) and for categorising the first example as 'dramatic playing' in which pupils engage spontaneously and which, crucially, they do not have to be taught.

We will return to this discussion in later chapters because it requires more exploration than is given here, but the example goes some way to illustrating how a seemingly straightforward question has hidden dimensions with theoretical implications. A reader might expect a book entitled *Starting Drama Teaching* to offer practical suggestions for lessons and lists of drama games and exercises. However, practical ideas are in themselves not enough because without an understanding of the rationale that underpins those practical ideas, the newcomer to the subject will inevitably flounder. Theoretical perspectives are needed but so too are insights into the way approaches to the subject have changed over the years.

Drama, perhaps more than many other subjects, can easily lend itself to an emphasis on practical activity without accompanying rationale. There is no shortage of purely practical books on drama teaching full of suggestions for activities, games and exercises but often devoid of a sense of purpose. Such books are only of value if one is able to discriminate adequately on the basis of sound aims and principles. Books which offer only practical suggestions are not so much devoid of theory but are driven by an implicit idea that being active and busy in the classroom is all that really matters. To borrow a phrase from Sartre, we are

Introduction

In one corner of an infant classroom a small group of pupils is busy playing. One is pretending to be a doctor, another a nurse and two are patients. One of the patients is being 'bandaged' and the other is having his temperature taken. In the secondary school nearby a drama class is taking place with a group of eleven-year-olds. Their drama is based on the story of the Pied Piper and in pairs the pupils are improvising a very simple scene in which two neighbours have mixed feelings of embarrassment and relief when they discover that both have an infestation of rats. Elsewhere in a theatre a group of professional actors is in the final stages of rehearsing a scene from *King Lear*.

Each of these activities could come under the umbrella concept of 'drama' used in its broadest sense. However, if we wanted to divide the activities in some way, which two have more in common? Which two activities have a 'family resemblance' and which is the odd one out? Of course there is no correct answer because it depends on what criteria we invoke. It would not be wrong to say that the first two have more in common because they take place in schools, although that would be a fairly superficial categorisation. Another approach is to argue that the first and second cases are examples of 'drama' (seen as creative, self-expression) and the work on *King Lear* is an example of 'theatre' (involving acting and performing). Or it is possible to say that the first two belong together because the pupils are not working from script. However, there is a less obvious but compelling case to be made for grouping the Pied Piper and the *King Lear* examples as instances of 'drama as an art form' (involving the conscious crafting of meaning) and for categorising the first example as 'dramatic playing' in which pupils engage spontaneously and which, crucially, they do not have to be taught.

We will return to this discussion in later chapters because it requires more exploration than is given here, but the example goes some way to illustrating how a seemingly straightforward question has hidden dimensions with theoretical implications. A reader might expect a book entitled *Starting Drama Teaching* to offer practical suggestions for lessons and lists of drama games and exercises. However, practical ideas are in themselves not enough because without an understanding of the rationale that underpins those practical ideas, the newcomer to the subject will inevitably flounder. Theoretical perspectives are needed but so too are insights into the way approaches to the subject have changed over the years.

Drama, perhaps more than many other subjects, can easily lend itself to an emphasis on practical activity without accompanying rationale. There is no shortage of purely practical books on drama teaching full of suggestions for activities, games and exercises but often devoid of a sense of purpose. Such books are only of value if one is able to discriminate adequately on the basis of sound aims and principles. Books which offer only practical suggestions are not so much devoid of theory but are driven by an implicit idea that being active and busy in the classroom is all that really matters. To borrow a phrase from Sartre, we are 'condemned' to theory in the sense that our practice and practical suggestions always carry implicit theoretical positions. If that is the case, it makes sense that theory should be examined explicitly rather than be taken for granted.

That does not mean of course that the main focus of this book will be theoretical; if practice without theory is in danger of being reductive, theory without practice can easily become vacuous and irrelevant. It is something of a cliché that theory and practice should be integrated and mutually enriching, easier to assert theoretically than to demonstrate in practice. For it is not obvious what form descriptions of practice should take in a publication of this kind. Detailed accounts of highly successful lessons which are intended to be inspirational can all too easily carry a subtext which celebrates the expertise of the author but serves to disempower the reader and make the fulfilment of similar goals seem unattainable. Human nature is such that it is all too tempting when giving retrospective accounts of drama lessons to embellish successful, moving moments by focusing on individuals who were most actively involved and ignoring the substantial numbers of pupils who were disengaged. On the other hand, accounts of lessons which simply offer structures without particular contextual details run the risk of ignoring the important considerations and decisions which ensured success. There are inevitably tensions involved in trying to write about teaching in a way that is of some practical help.

Learning to teach is a subtle process that involves gradually accommodating and assimilating ideas to one's own values, beliefs and personality. Very often newcomers to teaching have a cognitive grasp of the way they wish to be in the classroom but, despite the conceptual sophistication of their ideals, are often disappointed to find the only way they can begin to operate is to imitate the way they themselves were taught. There are numerous books on educational management and classroom discipline based on the erroneous assumption that the only requirement for success is to be told what to do. Teaching, like drama, is as much about feeling as it is about cognitive understanding; above all, it is never merely about the acquisition of skills. A book of this kind will be helpful only if it retains some sense of the, sometimes harsh, reality of what it is like to be in the classroom.

Most teachers know very well, however, that to take someone else's lesson plans or ideas and try to use them uncritically can lead to disaster. Sometimes examples of drama lessons simply take too much for granted. Attempts to translate ideas into practice which produced such solemn and committed approaches in the literature can often end up with pupils giggling, embarrassed or simply alienated or bored. Another reason why it is difficult to share practical ideas is that writers inevitably draw from their own specific cultural contexts; lessons that seemed appropriate in suburbs may not translate so easily into the inner city. We have probably all been in the position of reading practical advice that seemed to bear no relation to our own teaching situation. Such observations do not make it undesirable or pointless to give practical ideas but suggest that they should be read with an awareness of the limitations of applying them in an unthinking fashion. Very often in a subject like drama, ideas which are described in purely practical terms do not work for the reader because there is a lack of real conviction derived from an understanding of their purpose and value.

To illustrate this it might be helpful to indicate the ways in which an extremely simple, practical idea can go wrong. The detective game is one that I have used frequently as a gentle introduction to role play with classes of all ages and abilities. It is so simple and captivating that it is tempting to recommend it as foolproof but of course there is no such thing. The game works quite simply. The teacher takes the role of a detective who is questioning a suspect about a crime in order to break the alibi. The whole class rather than a single individual takes the role of the suspect and each person who is asked a question by the teacher has to keep the answer consistent with what has gone before. Thus a typical exchange might go as follows:

TEACHER: Where were you at 8.00 p.m. last Saturday?
PUPIL 1: On my way to the pub.
TEACHER: What time did you get there?
PUPIL 2: About 8.30 p.m.
TEACHER: Did you go with anyone?
PUPIL 3: I was on my own . . .

The teacher continues to question the pupils, trying to show that their alibi is false, for example: 'You just said you left the pub at 8.30 but a while ago you said that was the time you arrived . . .' The game is a very gentle introduction to the adoption of role (the pupils answer in the first person as if they are the subject) which can very easily be extended so that a character from a novel or a figure from history can be questioned in the same way about their attitudes and motives. Pressure is placed on one individual only for a very short period of time; there is little time for anyone to feel exposed or embarrassed. Nevertheless it does contain an element of tension which is an essential prerequisite of drama; one does not know when the alibi is going to crumble.

It demands that pupils listen to each other carefully and thus creates an appropriate atmosphere of concentrated attention which is warranted by the activity rather than externally imposed. The game can work only if the class unite as a cohesive group and, given the social nature of drama, this is a valuable preliminary exercise.

What then might go wrong with such a very straightforward game? The questioning by the teacher which at first sight appears unproblematic actually requires quite a subtle balance so that the questions are neither too easy (in which case the activity lacks any tension that the alibi might be broken) nor too difficult (in which case the particular individual or the class as a whole might be made to feel stupid). The way the game is introduced, particularly to older pupils, is important lest they feel patronised or silly. Some adolescents may feel that games in their classrooms are inappropriate no matter how much they actually enjoy them and may need to be told that the game will lead to an activity which will help everyone's understanding of the short story they are about to read.

A common problem in drama is that activities initiated by the teacher are simply not taken seriously. Imagine in this case that in answer to the first question 'Where were you at 8.00 p.m. last Saturday?' the reply comes back 'on the moon'. Because the motivating quality of the game relies on willing cooperation, it is not necessarily going to help if the teacher becomes cross and insists on serious answers. In that case the real game might become 'let us see how much we can annoy this teacher'. Nor is it necessarily helpful to treat the suggestion with deadly seriousness if that is likely to strain belief too much. In this case it might result in the teacher becoming the object of the joke; the game now becomes 'let's have a laugh at teacher's expense who accepts any old rubbish'. Much depends on what was intended by the answer in the first place; while this can be difficult to discern, it is unwise to jump to conclusions. In such circumstances it might be better to go along with the 'joke' for a short while and then ask for the game to be played again this time with a different tone. Unless one knows the precise context, the nature of the relationship with the class, the social dynamics of the group, it is difficult to suggest a course of action which will guarantee success. On the other hand, sensitivity to contextual considerations can lead to paralysis and a reluctance to give any practical advice at all. In this example it is possible to offer some general suggestions which are not so much rules of thumb but observations designed to highlight and anticipate particular problems which might arise:

- Try to get the right balance so that the questions are challenging but not impossible to answer.

- Question pupils in random fashion so that they are kept alert.

- Consider presenting the activity to older pupils as an introduction to role play rather than as a game.

- Do not work out the details of the crime in advance.

- Start to elevate the game into role play by interspersing the questions with phrases such as 'are you sure you are telling the truth?'

- Treat inappropriate responses lightly but ask for the game to be played more seriously the next time.

In the example given here some of the considerations pertain to drama (the need for the role play exercise to have an element of tension), others have more to do with general teaching issues (the need for flexibility of response). Even the simplest of exercises should not be approached by the teacher in a mechanical, unthinking way.

This book then aims to provide:

- an introduction to the practice of teaching of drama;

- an insight into theoretical perspectives which underpin practice;

- a guide to the tensions and differences of opinion which have marked its history;

- a guide to further reading.

The book does not claim to be 'everything you always wanted to know about drama'. Because its sphere of reference is wide, it is necessarily limited in its discussion of any one issue or practical method. There are important drama-related activities – such as dance, puppetry, movement – upon which it barely touches. Other topics are introduced but not discussed in great detail. A book which tries to say something useful to both primary and secondary teachers, to teachers of drama as a separate subject as well as teachers of English and other subjects runs the risk of satisfying no one. The further reading sections therefore are important in giving more sources of practical ideas and more detailed discussions of theoretical issues and controversies within drama.

The divisions which dogged the teaching of drama in the past have largely given way to a more tolerant and accepting view. It is highly unlikely to hear drama teachers condemning 'theatre arts' (performance, rehearsing, acting, working from script) as might have been the case in the 1970s. Conversely there are few teachers or writers who are so wedded to traditional theatre practice that they do not see the potential for rich work drawn from an emphasis on process using role play and improvisation. There is far greater potential for integrating approaches to drama than is often realised. It is important not just to be tolerant of opposing views and approaches but to see the way in which they can be mutually enriching.

Chapter 1 will start with examples of contrasting drama lessons in order to give an outline of past differences of opinion about methodology, aims and the place of drama in the curriculum. The need for a synthesis which preserves the best aspects of different traditions in drama teaching is stressed.

Chapter 2 will consider the place of drama in the National Curriculum and in the National Literacy Strategy. The fact that drama is compulsory in the National Curriculum is a mixed blessing because it makes the battle for separate subject status at Key Stage 3 much harder and inspection findings suggest that drama in the primary school is often neglected. Drama is a powerful teaching methodology. On the other hand, it is necessary to identify the distinctive but complementary nature of drama when identified as a separate subject.

Chapter 3 will offer suggestions on planning for drama (both lessons and schemes of work). Teachers who are new to drama often make the same sort of mistakes which are made by pupils when planning drama, for example a tendency to think solely in terms of narrative without sufficient attention to important elements of the art form.

Chapter 4 shows that even a simple activity such as setting up pairs role play is more complex than many publications assume. Many textbooks (of English and other subjects) end a section of activities with the simple instruction to 'improvise' or 'role play', making it sound as if it really is as easy as that. This chapter will in addition offer suggestions on the purposeful and selective use of games and exercises.

Chapter 5 will offer a guide to ways of categorising drama activities. An appropriate choice of activity (making a play up in groups, working in pairs, performing, using a particular convention) will depend on the aims of the teacher, the content of the lesson, and the experience of the class and the teacher. This chapter will also explore the practical implications of conceptual differences between concepts like 'drama' and 'dramatic play'.

Chapter 6 will aim to avoid undue repetition of what others have written but will explore what are now fairly familiar drama techniques from the point of view of the teacher who is new to the subject. Seemingly straightforward activities (questioning in role, the use of tableau), which are so valuable across the curriculum, can easily go wrong if approached in an inappropriate way. It is important to avoid an episodic and mechanical approach to using conventions. Suggestions will also be given on how the repertoire of techniques can be extended as teachers become more confident and how the inexperienced teacher can prepare for unexpected results.

Chapter 7 will look at drama in relation to play text, poetry and prose. This chapter will explore the reasons why play scripts were neglected in the past and will give examples of working with script in the drama lesson. It will also consider ways of using drama to explore writing of different kinds and the theoretical underpinning provided by literary theoretical perspectives.

Chapter 8 will examine the place of performance in the lesson as well as in the context of the wider culture of the school. The concept of acting and its absence from much of the writing on school drama will be considered. The importance of developing pupils' ability to respond to drama will also be discussed.

Chapter 9 will consider the problems involved in describing progression in drama and will emphasise the need to describe achievement in ways which do not reduce the subject to a mechanistic acquisition of skills. The problems involved in assessing drama will also be addressed.

Chapter 10 will focus on the concept of drama as art. Concepts of 'internal' and 'external' action will be considered with a view to identifying some of the mistakes made in the past by exponents of the subject.

Appendix A contains a full transcript of a twenty-minute sustained piece of dramatic play involving a four-year-old, which is referred to in several earlier chapters.

1

Teaching drama: balancing perspectives

Two drama projects

'THE PIED PIPER' is a common focus for drama at both Key Stages 2 and 3. Before describing contrasting drama approaches using the poem as a starting point (Projects A and B) it might be helpful to give a brief reminder of the story on which it is based. A city is so plagued with rats that the townspeople complain to the mayor. The Pied Piper is promised payment if he rids the town of the rats, which he does successfully by playing his musical pipe. When he is refused the promised payment his revenge is to charm the children of the town away with his music. They all follow him to a gap in the mountainside through which they disappear. One lame boy who cannot keep up is left behind.

In Project A the story has been set in a modern context and has been used to focus on a number of social and moral issues. The pupils have adopted different roles and improvised various scenarios: as residents of an estate they have complained to the council about the infestation of rats; in pairs they have enacted a scene in which the modern Pied Piper confronts the mayor to demand his rightful payment; they have enacted a council meeting in which different parties have argued over paying the debt; they have adopted the roles of families who have lost their children. In the course of the drama the teacher has also adopted roles, guiding the drama from the inside. Both within the drama and in discussion outside it they have considered the difficulties people have to confront when faced with an unresponsive bureaucracy, the way people are prone to self-deception when making moral decisions, and the way a town might be affected by a major catastrophe of some kind. The fact that the starting point has been 'The Pied Piper' is in some ways irrelevant – it is a convenient focus for the themes which have been the subject of the lesson.

In Project B the story has been enacted from a play text based on the poem and the drama has included the use of masks, costume, lighting and movement. In this example the pupils have not adopted different roles but they talk about having a 'part' in the play which they keep throughout the project. The acting of the story is carefully rehearsed with attention to such matters as voice projection, tone, stage design and the appropriate position and movement of the characters at various points in the production. The teacher has taken the role of director but has involved pupils in decisions about the appropriate staging of the story. Eventually the play will be performed for a small audience of invited parents and the final product will be impressive.

It will be clear from these descriptions that there are different orientations in the work described and readers who have any familiarity at all with drama teaching will recognise the representation in concrete terms of some of the major differences of emphasis which have been part of drama's history: drama/theatre, process/product, drama in education/drama education. The reader may already feel a particular affinity with one or other of the approaches and may be expecting here a critical attack on one of the two ways of working. Let's pause, however, and consider that the descriptions given above were of what most people would describe as successful versions of both approaches. That is not to say that everyone would necessarily agree with the implicit educational aims. It might be argued that the first project seems to embody the idea that the way to get results is to mount polite, restrained 'middle class' protests; why not demonstrate in the drama that rats are a product of poverty which in turn is a function of a capitalist economy? The second example seems to embody a very traditional and formal view of theatre. Both projects could be described as successful in their own terms. It is tempting in drama, and a generally recognisable trait of human nature, to compare a successful account of one's own preferred methodology with an unsuccessful account of the approach with which one disagrees. Yet the results can lead to distortion when it comes to theorising. It might be helpful then, in the interest of fostering an open mind to the more general issues, to consider in the case of each project what a highly unsuccessful attempt at drama might have looked like.

Project A has fairly rapidly disintegrated into chaos. Instead of the animated exchange between the residents and the mayor which took place on the in-service course from which the idea came, the children have started to shriek and stamp on imaginary rats. Others have decided they would like to be rats and have started to squeak and make rat-like faces. At the back of the group a rat and resident start to fight, the rat seeming to have acquired the ability to execute fancy karate moves. When the teacher moves to the representation of a town bereft of children, several groups think it is great fun to have a party to celebrate the fact and there is much miming of pulling champagne corks and drinking. When describing the lesson later to a colleague the teacher explains how some of the residents 'really got quite involved' and that the class 'seem to enjoy their drama very much'. Later, in a more reflective moment, the teacher ponders on the irony that one of the central themes of the lesson was intended to be self-deception.

Of course Project B can likewise be subject to a negative account. The work here has not been a disaster but it has been arid and uninspired. The pupils have delivered their lines for the umpteenth time in a stilted and slightly embarrassed manner. The fairly pushy characters in the class have been given the central parts and the rats have spent several lessons doing very little while they wait for the stars to rehearse. The voices of the participants can be heard but what little interest there was in the content of the work has been eroded by repeated attempts to get it right to the teacher's satisfaction. Fortunately the audience will be made up of parents who would be moved to tears if the pupils merely stood on one leg for the duration of the play, particularly if they manage to wave from the stage, a goal which most of them will be bent on achieving. On this occasion audience reaction is not the way to gauge the quality of the work or the value of the project.

The description of the two disasters, even though they are parodies, is a reminder that the claims and counter claims which were common in writing about drama and which were often couched in theoretical terms (or at best based on idealised accounts of practice) need to be balanced by an injection of pragmatism. Different approaches can have different degrees of success and insufficient attention has been paid in drama writing to determining what counts as success and quality irrespective of the particular drama mode; in the past many writers assumed that quality attaches to one or other particular approach to the subject. Interestingly enough, a similar diagnosis of what was wrong can be applied to both projects: insufficient belief in the fiction, no real sense of dramatic form, little understanding of the content.

Before examining some of the controversies that have dogged the history of drama teaching, it is easy to see that the two different projects could have been enriched by using ways of working more often associated with the alternative approach. The successful version of Project A has a clear focus on significant content in terms of moral questions and social issues. The approach, however, is highly verbal and cognitive, without exploiting the full range of signing possibilities in drama. Conversely in Project B the approach to dramatic form is more wide-ranging but it is not apparent from the description here that enough attention has been given to ideas. A closer look at the underlying theoretical positions reveals that it is difficult to sustain any justification for such discrete approaches.

Drama/theatre

Traditionally 'theatre' has been taken to refer to the communication of meaning in performance whereas 'drama' has referred to the work designed for stage representation, the corpus of written plays (Elam 1980). Thus 'drama' in the context of English teaching has tended to be viewed as a separate literary genre alongside poetry and the novel. In the context of drama teaching, however, the terms have been used rather differently. Perhaps the most emphatic and widely quoted statement of the difference between drama and theatre was made by Way in 1967:

> . . .'theatre' is largely concerned with communication between actors and an audience; 'drama' is largely concerned with experience by the participants, irrespective of any function of communication to an audience.
>
> (Way 1967: 2)

At first sight it does seem that Projects A and B correspond respectively to Way's distinction between drama and theatre. However, a closer examination of the details of each project reveals a rather less simple picture. In Project A it may well have been the case that pupils several times observed and therefore formed an audience for one another's work. In the second example, although the project culminated in a performance, the early workshops and rehearsals may well have involved pupils in drama work without an audience as such. Writers on drama often recognised that the distinction between 'drama' and 'theatre' as defined by Way is not that clear cut and tended to employ terms like 'showing', 'presenting', 'making' and 'performing' to indicate that there are shades of difference. Pupils may not necessarily perform on stage but they will inevitably share work with one another in the drama studio. A complete drama project (as opposed to a single drama activity) might include elements of presentation and performance.

It is more appropriate to talk about different orientations in drama work rather than to employ rigid categories. Even when there is no overt sharing of work, participants form an audience for one another while actively engaged in the drama. When participants momentarily stop their active involvement in the drama they become observers of the action, but there is also an ongoing reflective element in drama in that all participants are simultaneously both spectators and performers. Thus even work which is not primarily oriented towards performance has three increasingly concealed audience elements within it: when groups stop to observe one another's work, when participants momentarily change from 'actor' to 'spectator', and when it is recognised that it is in the nature of drama for all participants to be simultaneously observers or 'percipients' of their own work. The degree to which participants are oriented towards performance varies with the type of work. There is clearly a difference between a spontaneous, pairs exercise in a workshop which no one is observing and a performance on stage. However, even in the pairs exercise participants are often creating meaning with a sense of how the work would look to an outsider.

It might be more fruitful to ask not so much whether there is an audience present but what effect this has on the quality of the experience of the participants. In the early days of drama in education, when there was strong opposition to the idea of performance, the ideal form of drama was judged to be a form of 'living through' improvisation in which all participants engaged spontaneously. It was often argued that the central distinguishing factor was the presence or otherwise of an audience. However, at the height of the purist experiential drama approach in the 1970s the subject was promulgated by demonstration lessons attended by walls of absorbed teachers, in effect forming an audience for the work. It is interesting to look back at an early film based on the work of Heathcote (*Three Looms Waiting*), which by any standards contains drama work of a very high quality, and observe not just the 'audience' in attendance but the significant presence of the camera, which in those days before the advent of compact camcorders would have been all the more intrusive. This film, famous for advancing the cause of experiential, 'living through' drama, could be equally judged as a very effective piece of theatre; the important point is that the physical presence of an audience did not detract from the quality of the work.

Much theoretical writing since the early 1980s has centred on whether the type of drama affects the quality of experience of the participants. The suggestion has been that when participants are engaged in more spontaneous, improvised work (traditionally called 'drama') their level of engagement and feeling will be more intense and 'genuine' than when they are performing on stage (traditionally called 'theatre'). These arguments will be considered in more detail in Chapter 8 where it will be argued that there is no theoretical justification for saying that one type of drama *necessarily* results in a particular quality of experience. Common sense tells us that priorities change to some degree when a group starts to think more about polishing work for performance, but decisions about the type of work need to be made from a pedagogic rather than doctrinaire standpoint. It is also important to acknowledge that debates of this kind were often conducted in the context of writing about education without sufficient acknowledgement that similar debates were being held in the theatre in the context of writing about acting.

Process/product

The distinction between process and product has been closely allied with the drama/theatre divide and is often seen as being synonymous with it. However, it does bring a different dimension to the analysis of drama because it frees us from the rather crude consideration of whether or not there is an audience present but focuses instead on the nature of the participants' engagement in the drama. It is a question of contrasting the attention to the creation of a finished product with the engagement in the activity itself, the drama process. Preference for the notion of process has tended to signal the belief that the educational value of the work largely resides in the negotiating, planning, thinking in which pupils engage as opposed to reliance on external authority implied in the notion of 'product', whether that be represented by a text or stage performance. Again it is tempting to see Project A as an example of process work whereas in B the pupils seem more focused on product, but again the distinction is not that simple.

A moment's reflection reveals that these two concepts are also rather more slippery than is often assumed. For in an active discipline like drama every end product contains a process within it and every process is in some sense a product. That enigmatic statement needs to be unpacked. In Project A let us imagine that the pupils are engaged in an improvisation with themselves as citizens confronting the teacher in role as councillor. They are confronting an obstructive bureaucrat, arguing the case for more help, defending themselves against accusations of causing the problem in the first place. We could argue that the value for the pupils here is that they are actively engaged in an ongoing process but it could be equally argued that what actually motivates them in their work is the sense of creating a product. All we have to do is to imagine that a particular scene is video-recorded and in one sense it is immediately transformed into a finished entity, a product. Pupils are always in their drama, whatever form it takes, working towards a product. In the same way, when they are actually engaged in a performance they are involved in a dramatic process. To preserve an exclusive distinction between process and product is sometimes like trying to distinguish the notion of a football match from playing football; it is as if someone denies any ability to talk about the score or to identify the key player of the match on the grounds that they were only involved in the process. This example highlights the fact that it is not so much the choice of concepts we use which is important but the *consequences* of their use. The important question in drama is to ask whether an exclusive preference for one or other concept closes our mind to possibilities. For example, proclaiming that one is solely interested in process may result in a denial of possibilities of judging the quality of the 'product', making any form of evaluation extremely difficult. Conversely an exclusive preoccupation with product may result in a failure to see that the process is central to the overall quality of the educational experience.

A clearer distinction between the two concepts has been advanced by O'Toole (1992) when he argues for drama in education as a particular and distinctive genre. While acknowledging that process/product relate to each other on a continuum, he defines process in drama as 'negotiating and renegotiating the elements of dramatic form, in terms of the content and purposes of the participants' (ibid.: 3). In the context of 'living through' drama described above, an essential element in drama in education was that the participants do not know in advance what the outcome of the work will be. Some writers choose to distinguish between 'enactment' and 'improvisation' such that improvisation does not just mean 'making it up as you go along' but 'making it up with an unknown outcome'. Thus, in Project A it would matter crucially whether the pupils knew the story of the Pied Piper because in that case they would be working towards a known outcome. Decisions taken within the drama such as whether to confront the mayor, whether to promise payment to the Pied Piper and then renege on the promise would all be up to the participants themselves.

Now this form of drama in which the participants appear to make real, spontaneous decisions as the work progresses was thought by many exponents to be the ideal form of drama in education in which real learning or understanding takes place as opposed to other forms which merely consolidate what is already known. Many of the lessons described in the account of Heathcote's work which was written by Wagner in 1976 have this quality, and some of the results are outstanding. This approach to drama will be discussed more fully in Chapter 5 but it is worth making one or two comments at this stage. It is not always easy to distinguish what exactly it is which motivates such decisions taken within the drama. Quite often when the participants appear to be making a decision in response to a particular moral dilemma what is actually happening is that decisions are being taken with the primary intention of advancing the drama. It is therefore often the progress of the drama which determines the result of the choice. Thus in the Pied Piper lesson if the townspeople acquiesced to the mayor's refusal to do anything about the rat problem or if they decided to pay the Pied Piper, the play would come to a halt. Other dilemmas common in such improvised dramas, such as whether to invade the neighbouring tribe, to join the expedition which will go to another planet, may likewise be taken with more attention to the progress of the play than the moral consequences of the action. Of course that hardly matters if one's primary concern is the creation of the drama, but the educational claim has often been that pupils confront real decisions within the work. The intention here is not to debunk all descriptions of lessons in which 'real' decisions appear to be made but simply to urge a note of caution that all may not be what it seems.

One way of isolating the notion of process is to focus on an approach to drama which concentrates exclusively on spontaneous, unplanned improvisation. However, few exponents of drama would wish to subscribe to such a narrow methodology which is so hard to sustain in practice. In most cases, as in Projects A and B, participants are engaged in a process in order to create a product. We can only make a full judgement about the educational value of Project B if we know more about the process: whether, for example, the pupils understood and thought about the content in relation to the form. In the same way it is very difficult to make any proper assessment of the work in A unless we think in terms of product.

Drama in education/drama education

There has been increasing recognition in recent years that acquisition of ability *in* drama is important, not just learning *through* drama. There is less consensus on how ability or skills in drama should be conceived. Thus at first sight it would be tempting to argue that in Project A the pupils are focusing on issues and are not learning about drama itself. The teacher whose lessons follow the pattern described here may be thought to be indifferent as to whether pupils actually get better at drama itself and whether such a notion has any real meaning. However, just as it was difficult to conceive of a lesson without some element of observation of the work of others, it is difficult to conceive of the lesson being taught successfully without what could be described as attention to drama skills. Take a simple pairs exchange between Pied Piper and the mayor. For it to succeed and for it to avoid turning into a slanging match or the sort of debacle described in the second version of the lesson, the pupils will need to be helped to find dramatic tension and constraint in the work, which could be described as a form of drama teaching *per se*. When the teacher adopts a role in the drama this could be seen as a form of modelling. There was much more teaching of skills (often in quite a subtle and even unconscious way) in what we might term 'content' or 'issues' based drama than was often assumed. Contemporary approaches to drama teaching tend to make these skills rather more explicit.

In Project B, where the emphasis seems to be primarily on drama skills, we cannot make the claim that content is ignored without first having more information. Let us imagine that there is an exchange in the script between mayor and Pied Piper. The emphasis here may be on how particular lines should actually be spoken but that sort of discussion ought to look at the content of the words and the likely feelings and motivation of the participants. It is only a very traditional, narrow model of theatre practice and parody of an approach to drama teaching which sees the teacher as an authoritarian director and the participants as mere mindless automatons.

At this point a summary might be useful. There have been many differences of opinion in drama teaching based on distinctions about approaches to drama. We should not allow language to deceive us into thinking that there is anything absolute or exclusive about the categories employed. Nor is it helpful simply to brush the distinctions aside. We make categories for a purpose and when we review how best drama should be taught in schools theoretical distinctions need to be unpacked to reveal the important issues which are embedded in them. Chasing distinctions in drama without reference to practice is to be condemned to a conceptual treadmill. But the conceptual distinctions may draw attention to important questions: when is it important and when is it unhelpful to place emphasis on performance? Is there a danger that preoccupation with product can minimise the educational significance of the work? Does an undue emphasis on process minimise the opportunities for assessment?

History of drama teaching

We are now in a position to look briefly at the way thinking about drama teaching has developed since the middle of the twentieth century. The developments can be summarised in Figure 1.1 which appears to show that there has been a long period of argument and debate which has brought us right back to where we started. But that would be a mistaken interpretation because the intervening years have brought us a much richer understanding of the concepts involved.

The separation of 'drama' and 'theatre' depicted in Figure 1.1 is generally thought to have begun in the 1950s. Although there were many notable drama practitioners at the turn of the century, drama in education is thought by many to have its origins in the work of Slade (1954) who recognised child drama as a separate art form as opposed to adult theatre. His work was characterised by respect for the creative ability of children and minimum intervention by the teacher. Previous manifestations of drama had included training in speech, mime and the acting of plays, but Slade's approach was characterised by a belief in the value of the spontaneous dramatic play of young children. Way's approach had the same theoretical origins but placed more of a focus on individual practical exercises. The work of Bolton and Heathcote in the 1970s revolutionised drama teaching in that far more attention was paid to content, the quality of the experience of the pupils and the role of the teacher in elevating the quality of the drama and defining the learning area. In the early days of their work, drama in education (as the particular approach to drama became known) was taken to refer to the spontaneous acting out of improvised plays, but the methodologies widened and developed over the years. There have been many contemporary writers and practitioners in their tradition who have developed the subject in significant ways. In more recent years Hornbrook (1991, 1998) has criticised some of the widely accepted orthodoxies of drama in education.

Such is the account which tends to be written, but of course it contains simplifications. Slade was not anti-theatre but saw theatre as coming at the end of a developmental stage. Way's work did not consist exclusively of exercises. Most importantly the work of Bolton and Heathcote has never really stood still and many of the criticisms of their approach failed to acknowledge the development in their thinking. The significant influence of the Theatre in Education movement which was closely associated with the development of drama in education is often ignored in histories of developments in drama teaching or in discussion of the relationship between drama and theatre. Accounts of drama in education then are often highly selective and that needs to be borne in mind when considering past and contemporary criticisms.

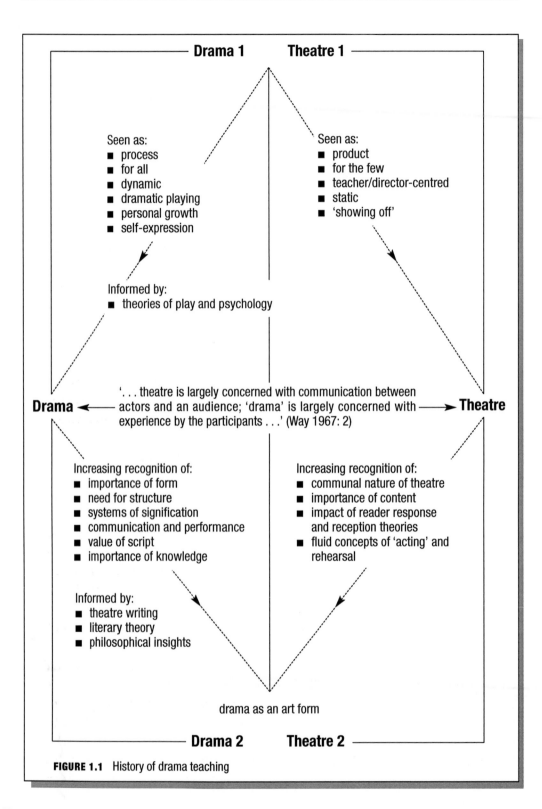

Drama 1   **Theatre 1**

Seen as:
- process
- for all
- dynamic
- dramatic playing
- personal growth
- self-expression

Seen as:
- product
- for the few
- teacher/director-centred
- static
- 'showing off'

Informed by:
- theories of play and psychology

Drama ← '... theatre is largely concerned with communication between actors and an audience; 'drama' is largely concerned with → **Theatre** experience by the participants ...' (Way 1967: 2)

Increasing recognition of:
- importance of form
- need for structure
- systems of signification
- communication and performance
- value of script
- importance of knowledge

Increasing recognition of:
- communal nature of theatre
- importance of content
- impact of reader response and reception theories
- fluid concepts of 'acting' and rehearsal

Informed by:
- theatre writing
- literary theory
- philosophical insights

drama as an art form

Drama 2   **Theatre 2**

FIGURE 1.1 History of drama teaching

One criticism of the drama in education tradition as practised through the 1970s and 1980s is that it lost its roots with dramatic art (Hornbrook 1998a). It was often a source of great confusion to the newcomer to drama teaching or indeed to the outsider to be told that drama in education has little to do with acting, theatre, the stage and play scripts which are, after all, those aspects of drama which are most normally associated with the subject. At the time when the separation of 'drama' and 'theatre' was happening what was being rejected was the negative aspects of theatre practice (depicted in the upper right side of Figure 1.1) when imposed prematurely on young people. In fact the unsuccessful description of drama Project B is an indication of some of the worst aspects of what this was thought to entail: little understanding of content and the encouragement of exhibitionism. What is interesting of course is to realise that later drama in education methods which were positively antagonistic to theatre practice were no guarantee that pupils would be involved and committed. There has been a tendency to elevate method to the status of principle instead of pursuing quality in whatever form it takes.

It is necessary to be aware of a conceptual sleight of hand in the argument that drama in education has lost its roots with dramatic art. It is one thing to argue that drama did lose its connection with theatre practice – which while only partially true (as stated above it ignores the significant contribution of theatre in education) is a question which can be subject to empirical investigation. However, it is another matter altogether to claim that drama lost its roots with art – which is more a matter of judgement and value. Most drama in education practitioners would argue that the whole history of the movement has actually been an attempt to reinstate art and aesthetic experience in drama work in schools. (Bolton (1979), for example, has argued that his work embodies elements of theatre form such as symbol, time, space.) The mistake made in the early days of drama in education of placing too much faith in one method (spontaneous improvisation) irrespective of quality of experience can also be made in assuming that the reinstatement of acting in scripted plays will automatically guarantee engagement in art.

Another more practical criticism of drama in education is that it has not been sufficiently aware of the realities of day-to-day classroom teaching. Hornbrook (1998a: 15) has argued there is a 'disturbing gap between the received wisdom of the field as broadcast in the literature and the actual experience, favourable and unfavourable, of the average school drama class'. The description of Project A at the start of this chapter was in marked contrast to that of the second unsuccessful lesson which rapidly descended into chaos. The best examples of drama in education practice which were often observed in demonstration lessons were difficult to sustain in the day-to-day reality of the classroom. Many teachers will recognise the force of that view. Teachers were facing a tall order if they expected to sustain week after week improvised work of the high quality which they may have observed on video or on courses.

Perhaps the most telling criticism of drama in education is that achievements in drama have been impossible to evaluate. If one is using drama to teach other subjects then it is a relatively easy matter to evaluate its success because the evidence will be provided by the pupils' increased understanding of the subject concerned. The problem is more difficult in the context of drama as a separate subject. If the claim is made that the purpose of drama is to further learning, it makes sense to ask what that learning has entailed and this is where drama in education has been at its weakest.

Critics have been quick to point to the inadequacy of attempts to describe achievements in drama when couched in those terms. This is a complex question which will receive more attention in Chapter 2. In any successful drama lesson there may be a number of achievements – development of personal qualities such as increased self-confidence, development of a greater understanding of the content, development of language and development of understanding of and ability in drama. The appropriate question to ask is which of these should be emphasised in formulating objectives and in making evaluative judgements. Arguments which for the purposes of assessment focus attention on the ability to operate within the conventions of drama are compelling but it must not be assumed that in doing so questions about understanding of content have been shelved in the process.

Neelands' writing has quite rightly been admired for its impact on the practice of drama in schools in making complex ideas accessible to teachers. His work on conventions will be explored more closely in Chapter 6. His writing on theatre deserves equal acknowledgement for he has been one of the main voices drawing attention to the fact that an understanding of changing conceptions of theatre is important in illuminating drama teaching in schools (Neelands 1998: viii). What was being rejected at Theatre 1 in Figure 1.1 was a very negative conception of theatre practice with authoritarian director, mindless actors as automatons and superficial use of theatre craft (costume, lights, etc.). Words like 'rehearsal' and 'acting' were banished from the drama teacher's vocabulary. Those who had entered teaching from degree courses in theatre (rather than English) often had to abandon much of what they had learned and acquire a new vocabulary and new way of thinking. However, the concept of Theatre 2 in Figure 1.1 is richer than Theatre 1. This theme will be explored in Chapters 7 and 8 but a simple example here might help explain the difference in emphasis: a rehearsal as conceived in terms of Theatre 2 is likely to incorporate many of the techniques normally associated with 'drama in education' or 'process' work.

Figure 1.1 also indicates the changes in the way theoretical ideas underpinned drama practice. At the point when concepts of drama and theatre were parting company, writers on drama tended to draw on theoretical writings on child play and psychology rather than on the theatre. The emphasis was on the personal growth of the individual through creative self-expression. But the changed conception at Drama 2 in Figure 1.1 means that all drama in the classroom can draw on insights provided by the nature of drama as art and writings from theatre practitioners. It now makes more sense at Drama 2 to talk about what 'teaching drama' involves (as opposed to just 'teaching though drama') without this being reductive, narrow or authoritarian. It also helps to bear in mind the advantages brought from still seeing drama in some respects as a form of play with regard to the pupils' level of absorption and engagement.

Balancing perspectives

A more balanced perspective has emerged since the early 1990s and there is now a far greater acceptance of varied approaches in the classroom, but that does not mean that there is no room for debate and differences of opinion. Norman (1999: 8), writing about the work he observed after an absence from the drama scene, commented that nothing he saw was 'inspirational, exploratory, owned, negotiated or characterised by participants working in the "here and now" of drama'. Such comments need to give pause for thought. The drive towards providing a knowledge base for the subject, clear objectives and predetermined structures for lessons can easily lead to work which is neither challenging nor engaging. These themes will be explored in subsequent chapters.

The notion of 'balancing perspectives' is ambiguous in that it refers not just to balancing opposing sides but also to getting each set of arguments into proper perspective. A balanced perspective has the following characteristics:

- It acknowledges that successful drama cannot be taught in a formulaic and mechanistic way but it involves creative energy and risk taking.

- It recognises drama both as a separate subject and an educational method, as having a valuable contribution to make to other curriculum areas. The opportunities for collaboration between drama and other subject teachers should be exploited.

- It seeks to establish what the distinctive elements of drama as a separate curriculum subject entail. This involves taking a broad view of the subject to include work on scripted text, the value of performance, the importance of focusing on the ability to respond to drama.

- It acknowledges the fact that particular emphases in drama may be appropriate for particular ages.

- It sees a place for performance as appropriate without denying that a different sort of emphasis is placed when pupils engage in a performance as opposed to drama workshops.

- It recognises that asking participants in drama to engage prematurely in performance runs the risk of inviting superficial work.

- It recognises the importance of evolving criteria for evaluating achievement in drama which are not based purely on superficial aspects of work.

- It seeks to integrate elements drawn from different traditions.

This chapter will end as it began with examples of drama activities based on the Pied Piper theme. They will be described here in order to illustrate the degree to which education *in* and *through* drama complement each other. But also to show the way in which process work can be integrated with work on script and more focused performance. In practice, the activities would be combined to form a more extended project on the theme.

1   After reading the poem, pupils are asked by the teacher to identify five scenes which would summarise the poem or five illustrations to accompany it in a book. Each group then takes one of the agreed scenes and forms a frozen image or tableau to represent the picture. (This technique will be explained in more detail in Chapter 6.) The first activity is one of comprehension, of judging priorities and selecting key moments in the story; the pupils are also implicitly beginning to consider the way narrative and dramatic forms differ. By creating a tableau they are learning about the use of space and signs to create meaning.

2   In pairs, pupils take the roles of two neighbours both of whom have a problem with rats but are too embarrassed to admit this to each other. Gradually the truth emerges in their conversation. In this activity the pupils are exploring a recognisable human trait of being conscious of appearances in social contexts. They are also learning that one of the ways in which dramatic dialogue develops is to include a level of significance which penetrates below the surface meaning of the words spoken.

3   The class in role as citizens of the town make representations to the mayor to get him to do something about the infestation. The teacher in role as mayor procrastinates and accuses them of not looking after their property. He tests their resolve and the pupils have to find the appropriate language and arguments to press their case. For the scene to work as drama they have to learn to listen to one

another's cues, to read the signs given by the teacher as the work develops. In other words they have to learn to accept and work with the conventions of the dramatic form. It may be difficult for the whole class to take part in the improvisation but a small group of representatives can be observed by the others in the class who offer comments on the way the scene should develop.

4 The teacher then asks the class to consider how a group of people might be able to break a promise and yet convince themselves that they are doing the right thing. Although some of the townspeople begin with moral scruples that the promise should be kept, in the course of a short meeting they change their mind. This sequence is difficult to improvise so the teacher breaks them into groups to work on short lines of script related to the theme of self-deception:

'I don't think he was expecting to be paid so much money.'
'He might have put the rats there in the first place.'
'Perhaps it was a coincidence that the rats left at the same time the Pied Piper went to work.'
'He surely did not expect to be paid that much.'
'He will be satisfied with a fraction of the amount.'
'He will understand that we need the money for important projects in the town.'

The class then combine their ideas into what amounts to a scripted performance.

5 It is now many months after the children of the town have left with the Pied Piper. The class are asked in groups to prepare, rehearse and perform a scene which shows a town bereft of its children. This is quite a challenging task requiring not a piece of purely naturalistic work but the creation of a symbolic scene which captures the appropriate degree of poignancy without sentimentality. The class will need help from the teacher to construct and develop their ideas. They need to know that the scene needs to be fairly simple and understated – for example, shops no longer sell sweets, the swings are being taken down in the park, a family look through their photograph album. By including in the scene someone who does not know the recent past history of the town there is potential here for learning about dramatic irony. They are given a definite (single) space in which to work and are restricted to a number of lines. They are asked to think about beginnings and endings and, depending on the experience of the group, use of costume, objects and light. A more general question can be posed about the staging of 'The Pied Piper' as a whole: how can theatre conventions be used to alter the mood to emphasise either the comic or sinister undertones (both of which are present in the poem)?

For different age groups the same starting point could be used to explore different thematic content as well as different drama approaches as represented in Table 1.1.

TABLE 1.1 Different approaches to 'The Pied Piper'

Age group	Thematic content	Drama focus
7+	Consequences of breaking a promise. Judging moral conduct: who was most at fault – the mayor or the Pied Piper?	Using mime and simple role play to convey narrative. Recognising different ways of conveying character (dress, actions, tone).
11+	How do we ensure citizens' rights are respected? Examining corruption among town officials. Exploring whether the child left behind had mixed feelings.	Whole-group improvisation. Creating scripted dialogue with subtext.
14+	Exploring influence of media on political decisions. Examining people's capacity for self-deception. Examining the mythical dimension – have the pupils passed through to a better world?	Experimenting with different dramatic structures and time frames. Examining the way the story might have been handled by different playwrights.

With older classes it is possible to explore in a fairly light-hearted way how different playwrights might have approached the story. As with all pastiche, the extracts do not replicate exactly the particular styles; for example, the Pied Piper story would hardly be appropriate subject matter for Greek tragedy.

Sophocles

The action of the play takes place in the mayor's chambers with the townsfolk acting as chorus. The play focuses on the day the children were taken by the Pied Piper. The previous history of the rats infestation and broken promises is given in various duologues. A messenger enters with news that the children have been taken.

MESSENGER: Hear, men of Hamelin, hear and attend.
You that have not seen,
And shall not see, this worst, shall suffer the less.
But I that saw, will remember, and will tell what I remember.
The Piper stood in mottled clothes
Of woven cloth and decked about with stars.
He put his pipe to lip and soft he blew
And lo from out each door there came
Child after child with cheeks aglow.
They skipped and danced with sprightly step.
I cried aloud, foreboding ill

'Unhappy children, stay and halt your step'.
But on they bound until they came
Before a rock in the mountain high.
A terrible sight arrested then my eyes . . .

Points to note: in Greek tragedy much of the action occurs off-stage and is reported; the use of verse; the use of direct speech within the messenger's speech; the portentous tone.

Shakespeare

The mayor has persuaded the council to break the promise to pay the Pied Piper. When the Piper leaves the chamber the mayor delivers a soliloquy in which he reveals his true motives.

Exit Piper

MAYOR: This is the excellent foppery of the world
That those in power do bend and sway with ease.
They hold me well – the better then my purpose work on them.
I know this Piper. He will exact a vengeance on this town
And seek a prize much higher than the first.
Then will I with furrowed brow and smooth dispose
Extract a payment from this town to quell the player's ire.
The Piper will as tenderly be led by the nose
As asses are.
He will to my house this night with outstretched hand
And with a bare bodkin I will despatch him thus.
This Piper will not the morrow see.

Points to note: the convention of direct address to the audience; the absence of explicit stage directions; the way the speech is used to further the narrative complication (the mayor plans to double-cross both the townsfolk and the Pied Piper).

Chekhov

Exactly two years have past since the Pied Piper took the children from Hamelin. The members of the council who were responsible for breaking the promise have tried to put the events behind them.

In the house of the Prokovs. Olga stands looking out of the window. Irina is sitting on a couch. On one wall is a picture of two smiling children. A rocking horse stands in the corner, dusty and dilapidated.

OLGA: It's exactly two years since they left. Two years ago today – May the fifth. I thought I should never survive it. But now here's two years gone by, and we can think about it again quite calmly. It was hot then just like it is today, hot and balmy.

(The clock strikes twelve)
The clock kept striking then, too.

(Pause)
I remember the music, the pipe playing. I remember them skipping and dancing.
IRINA: Why keep harking back?
OLGA: If only, if only I had at least spoken to them before they left.

Points to note: the use of stage directions; the use of dialogue to evoke mood; the setting in an ordinary household where the tensions from past events will surface.

O'Casey

The scene is a pub where some of the townspeople have been celebrating the fact that they did not pay anything for getting rid of the rats.

A public house at the corner of the street. One corner of the public house is visible to the audience. The counter covers two-thirds of the length of the stage. On the counter are beer-pulls and glasses. Behind the counter are shelves running the whole length of the counter. On these are rows of bottles. The barman is seen wiping the counter. To the left side of the stage is the street outside the bar which is in darkness. Micky is drinking at the bar. He is a small man of about thirty. He is wearing trousers and a check shirt with an ill-matching tie pulled to one side. It is an hour later.

BARMAN *(wiping counter)*: So he's gone without his money?
MICKY: I told, I told him the bowser, put your mitts up I said and I'll knock you into the middle of next week.
JIMMY: Be God, you put the fear o' God in him! I thought you'd have to be dug out of him. Him, with his pointy hat and the stoop of him.
MICKY: You'd see some snots flying if I belted him. He had us for a pack of goms thinking we'd pay him that much money. Sure didn't Furbo chase the rats from my house. I needed no piper. He was playing his tunes all the week and no rats came peeping out from their holes
JIMMY: He'll be gone now and we'll not see him again. He's off to try it on some other old fools.

The light dims on the pub and rises at the side of the stage. The pub goes silent although the townsfolk continue to mime as if they are talking; they are unaware of what is happening outside. The plaintive sound of a pipe can be heard which gets gradually louder. The Pied Piper appears and moves right with a group of children following him.

Points to note: the detailed stage directions; the contrast in mood and action between the more comic goings-on in the bar and the happenings outside; the colloquial language and style.

Pinter

We find ourselves in the home of the Pied Piper.

A living-room. A gas fire down left. Kitchen door up right. Table and chairs centre. A double bed protrudes from alcove. Door leading to the hall down left.

Pete enters from the door on the left and sits at the table. He takes a musical instrument, a pipe, from his pocket and holds it to his lips. He stops, changes his mind and puts it back in his pocket. He picks up a paper and starts to read.

Angie enters with a plate and puts it in front of him.

ANGIE: Here you are. This will warm you up.
(*She turns the gas fire down*)
ANGIE: Anything good?
PETE: What?
ANGIE: Anything nice?
(*Pause*)
PETE: I need to try it again.
(*Pause*)
ANGIE: Something will turn up.
(*He reads the newspaper*)
PETE: Someone's just had a baby.
ANGIE: Oh, they haven't. Who?
PETE: Lady Mayoress.
ANGIE: Is it a girl?

Points to note: the blend of naturalism with an air of mystery; the ordinary domestic setting; the use of silences and pauses to suggest subtext.

Bennett

The play takes place in the home of the town clerk. He lives with his mother.

Graham is a middle-aged man. The play is set in his bedroom, a small room with one window and one door.

I can't say the service was up to scratch. Mother likes bone china not those mugs with the thick rims. And the crumpets were a bit stale. They think you can't tell when they toast them. Mother likes to take her teeth out when she's eating crumpets – she says it's better for sucking out the butter. I said, 'Mother you'll shame me.' She said, 'You watch it or you'll not have any teeth yourself.' She likes a bit of a joke but she knows when to draw the line. We laughed that time when she cut my lip. Anyway we had a bit of a do at the council today. The chap that got rid of the rats came back for his money. He still looked a sight. I don't know where he bought his raincoat but it was a bit bright for my taste. We made the right decision not to pay him. As mother said last night, 'nothing's binding except in writing'.

Points to note: the use of monologue; the use of direct speech within the monologue; the exposition through speech; the use of subtext with the words conveying more than the speaker is aware.

For the newcomer to drama the examples of extracts from lessons in this chapter are likely to raise all sorts of practical questions: how does one go about introducing tableau to pupils who have not done this type of work before? What if pupils cannot think of anything to say when they are asked to role play? What if they start to giggle? Such questions will be the subject of discussion in subsequent chapters.

Further reading

Full details of titles are given in the Bibliography.

For a detailed history of drama teaching see Bolton, G. (1998) *Acting in Classroom Drama*. Different perspectives on teaching drama are to be found in books by Hornbrook, D. (1998a) *Education and Daramatic Art* and Bolton, G. (1992a) *New Perspectives on Classroom Drama*. For a detailed discussion of drama as process see O'Toole, J. (1992) *The Process of Drama*. Readers who wish to delve more deeply into past divisions and differences in drama teaching might want to read articles by Clegg (1973), Mackay (1992), Davis (1991), Neelands (1991), Battye (1993), Abbs (1992), Bolton (1992b), Britton (1991), Wrack (1992). Earlier books which expressed some reservations about prevailing drama in education practice include Allen, J . (1979) *Drama in Schools: Its Theory and Practice* and Watkins, B. (1981) *Drama and Education*. Chapter One of Burgess, R. and Gaudry, P. (1985) *Time for Drama* provides an overview of the traditional drama/theatre divide.

2 Drama, the National Curriculum and the National Literacy Strategy

The place of drama in the curriculum

THERE IS A STRONG CASE to be made for drama both as a separate subject and as teaching methodology (drama across the curriculum). It is important, however, to consider the argument that the more drama is recognised as a teaching method the less claim it has to separate subject status. These arguments will be considered in relation to drama's place in the National Curriculum and Literacy Strategy.

When teachers and writers refer to the drama content in the National Curriculum they usually have in mind the use of drama strategies and conventions identified under the speaking and listening strand and tend not to include the study of Shakespeare and other play texts. The reasons for this can be seen from the discussion in the last chapter. Drama in the school context is often taken to refer to active forms of improvised role play and play-making rather than the study of literary texts. Drama both in its narrow and wider sense appears quite prominently in the National Curriculum. In addition to the content of the speaking and listening strand, Shakespeare is compulsory at Key Stage 3 as well as at Key Stage 4. Drama texts have to be read which extend pupils' 'moral and emotional understanding' as well as their understanding of drama in performance. Pupils' writing at both Key Stages is expected to include dialogues, play scripts and screenplays, using their experience of reading, performing and watching plays.

The previous chapter identified the different orientations in the history of drama teaching towards 'dramatic playing' on the one hand and 'theatre' on the other. It was also suggested that those categories are by no means clear cut. We can now add a third conceptualisation of drama as 'literary discipline' (the study of plays). These three categories are useful ways of seeing the development of thinking about drama teaching and of focusing on discussion on the role of drama in the curriculum. Drama in schools has variously been conceived:

- as a literary discipline
- as theatre
- as dramatic play.

Such categories, however, should not be seen as independent from each other and should not be translated into discrete forms of practice as often happened in the past. Plays were not written to be studied only as literary texts and such an approach tends to result in an examination of themes and characters rather than the creation of meaning in performance. A narrow concept of theatre assumes that the roles of playwright, actor, producer and audience have to be separate and the audience passive, and that the emphasis is all on surface action with no attention to meaning or understanding. To see drama only as 'dramatic playing' is to underestimate the importance of structure and form. Table 2.1 (adapted from Fleming 2001) highlights the strengths and weaknesses of each way of conceptualising drama.

TABLE 2.1 Ways of conceptualising drama

Drama as	Weakness	Strength
Literary discipline	Drama was written to be watched and performed, not studied passively from behind desks.	Places emphasis on content and gives balance to an approach which over-emphasises stagecraft at the expense of meaning.
Theatre	Danger of emphasis on empty experiences for pupils where the focus on acting, lighting, scenery does not take enough account of content.	Restores drama as a cultural, communal activity with its own distinct subject content. Emphasises responding to drama as well as performing.
Dramatic play	Lack of sufficient subject discipline means that it is often difficult to know what learning is going on. Difficult to assess or determine progression.	Pupils tend to be involved and engaged because the work is accessible. More potential for drama as teaching methodology.

The categories given in Table 2.1 also throw some light on discussions about the place of drama in the curriculum. Almost as much energy has been devoted to arguing about whether drama should be conceived as a 'subject' or 'method' as it has to the drama/theatre debate. It has been customary to see the category of 'drama as method' as referring to the use of role play, improvisation, and conventions such as hotseating and tableaux to teach other subjects. But drama in the context of English is rather more complex, combining elements of both subject and method. This insight has implications for the place of drama in the National Curriculum.

When the National Curriculum was first published in 1987, the failure to include drama as a separate foundation subject caused a considerable amount of shock and anger in the drama teaching world. Although writers on drama were united in their opposition to its exclusion, they did not agree on why that policy had been reached. Drama has been strengthened in the 2000 version of the English curriculum, but it still failed to secure separate subject status. Some claimed drama was excluded because of its radical potential as a subject in getting pupils to think for themselves. Other writers thought that drama exponents themselves could be held responsible because the emphasis on drama as teaching method undermined its status as a separate subject.

There is, however, a simpler explanation. To the uninformed, drama already existed as a genre within English alongside poetry and the novel, in the same way that dance could be seen to find its niche within PE. To argue that drama should occupy a separate place on an overcrowded curriculum would be likened by some to the claim that algebra should exist as a subject separate from maths. Those who advocate that drama should exist as a separate subject in the National Curriculum are faced with a dilemma. If drama is conceived less as a traditional subject with a body of knowledge and skills and more as a teaching and learning methodology then its claim to separate subject status is likely to fall on deaf ears in the present climate in which such a premium is placed on clear objectives and assessable outcomes. On the other hand, if drama is conceived in more traditional subject-specific terms its overlap with English reduces the impact of the argument for separate subject status. After all, English teachers are encouraged in the National Curriculum and by examination boards to treat plays as performance and not just literary texts.

Much of the writing in drama teaching since the 1960s has focused on teaching methodologies rather than on what might be described as the content of drama as a subject, but it has to be remembered that the conception of the curriculum as a collection of subjects and the notion of subject as a body of knowledge/content has not always been as much taken for granted as it is today. In the 1960s and 1970s – with the influence of sociology of knowledge, curriculum study and philosophy of education – the question of whether the curriculum should be conceived as a collection of subjects was by no means taken for granted and it is against that intellectual background that drama was developing.

Despite the narrow approach to the curriculum embodied in the demands of national testing, the early 1980s onwards has seen a huge change in teachers' understanding of and approach to children's learning. Fostered by philosophical and psychological perspectives, and disseminated by various forms of in-service training aimed at expanding teaching and learning styles, the challenge to a view of learning as being essentially passive has been considerable. The primary school from Plowden onwards has always been a more fertile ground for innovative approaches to learning. At secondary level the introduction of GCSE was an opportunity to affirm many of the changes in education which had been developing in previous years. At one stage it seemed that every educational initiative (including the use of drama) claimed exclusive ownership of the notion that learning is not a passive affair but involves the learner in the construction of knowledge. The concept of multiple intelligences, recognition that people have differences in learning styles, insights into learning derived from physiological study of the brain all offer strong arguments for drama as a powerful means of learning.

Although the literacy framework for Key Stages 1 and 2 does not contain a separate drama strand, several publications have sought to fill the gap by demonstrating ways in which the strategy can be enriched by the use of drama. There are specific references to (some fairly uninspiring) drama activities in the framework, some examples of which are given below (full summaries can be found in titles identified in the further reading section at the end of this chapter).

- *Year 1*: to re-enact stories in a variety of ways, e.g. through role play, using dolls or puppets.

- *Year 3*: to write simple playscripts based on own reading and oral work.

- *Year 4*: to chart the build-up of a play scene, e.g. how scenes start, how dialogue is expressed, and how scenes are included.

- *Year 5*: to evaluate the script and performance for their dramatic impact.

- *Year 6*: to prepare a short section of story as a script, e.g. using stage directions, location/setting.

A separate strand for drama (drawn from the National Curriculum) as identified in the framework for Key Stage 3 is summarised in Table 2.2.

TABLE 2.2 Drama in the Key Stage 3 Literacy Strategy

Year	Drama content
7	Develop drama techniques to explore in role a variety of situations and texts or respond to stimuli. Work collaboratively to devise and present scripted and unscripted pieces, which maintain the attention of an audience. Extend their spoken repertoire by experimenting with language in different roles and dramatic contexts. Develop drama techniques and strategies for anticipating, visualising and problem-solving in different learning contexts. Reflect on and evaluate their own presentations and those of others.
8	Reflect on their participation in drama and identify areas for their development of dramatic techniques, e.g. keep a reflective record of their contributions to dramatic improvisation and presentation. Develop the dramatic techniques that enable them to create and sustain a variety of roles. Explore and develop ideas, issues and relationships through work in role. Collaborate in, and evaluate, the presentation of dramatic performances, scripted and unscripted, which explore character, relationships and issues.
9	Recognise, evaluate and extend the skills and techniques they have developed through drama. Use a range of drama techniques, including work in role, to explore issues, ideas and meanings, e.g. by playing out hypotheses, by changing perspectives. Develop and compare different interpretations of scenes or plays by Shakespeare and other dramatists. Convey action, character, atmosphere and tension when scripting and performing plays. Write critical evaluations of performances they have seen or in which they have participated, identifying the contributions of the writer, director and actors.

As with so many initiatives of this kind, it is sometimes difficult for teachers to know what stance to take. It could be seen as a matter for some celebration that drama is given due acknowledgement in the framework. On the other hand, alongside all the other objectives and demands it is difficult to see its treatment as being more than perfunctory, nor is it sufficiently acknowledged that drama needs to be recognised as a specialism. There is no indication of how it is to be specifically taught to pupils. This is ironic. The strategy over-emphasises the explicit teaching of language, elevating the ability to parrot such terms as 'causal connective' at the expense of sensitivity to nuances of meaning, but underestimates the degree to which drama needs to be taught. The vacuum at the heart of the Literacy Strategy is a proper underpinning by a theory of language and meaning. The implicit assumption (conveyed in the training materials rather than the explicit rationale in the framework) is that language is transparent and can be easily reduced to lists of structures and objectives. Many English textbooks tag onto the end of a series of written tasks the rather lazy instruction to 'improvise in groups' with no other advice on helping pupils structure their work.

It is not necessary to see any conflict between justifications of drama as subject or method. However, what needs to be recognised is that to use drama effectively as teaching methodology requires an understanding of the art form just as when drama is taught as a separate subject. The mistake made in the past was to assume that knowledge in the case of drama consists of theatre history, stagecraft or literary criticism and that the ability to devise and structure drama is somehow innate because dramatic playing seems to come naturally. This is complex because there is a sense in which aspects of drama do come naturally but in that it is no different from other arts forms all of which can be said to have their origins in 'the bedrock of the spontaneous reactions that we make, from earliest infancy, to nature and created things' (Lyas 1997: 1).

A scrutiny of some of the reasons popularly advanced for the value of drama as pedagogic method reveals an implicit recognition of the nature of drama as an art form or subject. The discussion which follows will therefore examine some of the reasons advanced for the value of drama as a teaching method to reveal the underlying recognition of the deeper nature of drama as subject. In each case, examples will be drawn from uses of drama across the curriculum.

Drama provides motivation

A Year 7 teacher has been engaged in a project on the Vikings, focusing in particular on the discovery made at Sutton Hoo in 1939 when a tomb of a Viking king buried in a ship and accompanied by arms, weapons and treasures was uncovered. The class have read about the discovery and have performed various tasks in the classroom but interest is low and there is little sense of animation. The use of drama is introduced by inviting pupils to adopt the roles of specialist historians and archaeologists. They will have to imagine that the Sutton Hoo discovery has only fairly recently been made and they are being asked to offer a second opinion to corroborate the findings of an 'expert' (teacher in role) who is about to publish a book on the discovery. In the course of the lesson pupils examine photographs, take measurements, reconstruct the scene of the discovery and temporarily with-hold the actual knowledge they have in order for their scientific work to proceed and 'discoveries' to be made in the course of the drama. They address a number of questions pertaining to the find: why was the treasure still there when so many barrows had been robbed by earlier treasure hunters? Why was no body ever found? Why was treasure buried when someone died? The teacher knows that for the lesson to work as drama rather than mere simulation some tension needs to be injected. He attempts in role as the author to persuade the experts first of all to agree with his mistaken interpretations (he did not even recognise that this was the tomb of a king) and then to collude with him in repressing the truth. The pupils find themselves defending and articulating the intrinsic importance of establishing historical truth, having explored ways in which the past is recon-structed. They are also in the course of the drama examining the way historical interpretations depend on selection of sources and distinguishing between fact and point of view. As the class leave the lesson the inevitable comments after suc-cessful drama work ('that was great', 'can we do that next week'?) come in abundance. Notice that the original intention was not to use drama to introduce new knowledge but originally had the more modest aim of reviving a flagging project by increasing motivation. Seen as a contingent method, drama was one choice among many: a visit to a museum or watching a video might have had a similar effect. However, the very steps which were taken to help the drama to suc-ceed as drama brought a new dimension to the exploration of historical concepts.

At one level the effect of a successful drama on pupils' motivation could be explained because it provides a break from established classroom routines. While there may be some truth in that assertion, change in routine can be provided in a number of ways and this alone does not explain drama's special appeal. A more convincing explanation of drama's motivational force is that it harnesses the incli-nation to play which while at its strongest in early childhood persists into adolescence and arguably into the whole of adult life. The association of play and learning has a long history within educational thinking. Drama's early pioneers recognised that drama has its origins in the natural dramatic play of young chil-dren and can be associated with a tradition of educational reformers who promoted liberal/progressive approaches to education. Watkins (1981: 14) has pointed out that 'we preserve in the familiar theatrical expressions players, play-house, and the play, the relationship of drama to the whole world of Play and Game'. Both in the history of the theatre and the history of the individual play in the form of dramatic enactment there is both a source of recreational pleasure and a means of making sense of the world.

But drama is both play and not play. It is not easy to define when 'dramatic play' becomes 'drama' but it lies in the realm of content (when participants have to face up to the consequences of their actions) and form (when they are constrained by its demands). The distinction will be considered in more detail in Chapter 5. Playing at being archaeologists would have presented few barriers to them whatever treasure they wished to find and at whatever pace. When the pupils 'play' (in the dramatic sense) at being archaeologists they are limited and bound by the need to make a play which involves injecting shape and tension and the demands of the subject (the need to focus on some aspect of Sutton Hoo); the two are inextricably related. In primary school the potential for integrating a project of this kind with other areas of the National Curriculum is considerable: examination of the way historical events are depicted in art forms, reading of extracts on the burial of the king from *Beowulf* and the Roald Dahl story *The Mildenhall Treasure*, writing of a museum guide book to the treasure, drawing scale diagrams to depict the exact size of the longboat and working out how to calculate the original size of an object of this kind from the available remains, plotting the site of the Sutton Hoo discovery and other similar European finds on a map.

It is a concrete activity

Let us look at another very simple example of the use of drama. It is the first term of a new academic year and the PSHE teacher wishes to introduce a lesson on school rules and personal responsibility. There are a number of ways in which the topic could have been introduced, but today a simple piece of drama will be used to introduce the topic. The teacher invites a volunteer to work with her and with a minimum amount of planning (simply to tell the class that they are going to watch the acting out of an exchange between teacher and pupil) begins the simple pairs improvisation with the question, 'Why were you late again this morning?'

A hush descends on the class as they watch the very simple spectacle which will unfold before them. It will only last a matter of minutes and may then be subject to discussion (was the teacher's reaction reasonable?), modification (could we try it again with a different excuse this time? Could we try it again with the pupil this time giving the impression that she is telling lies?), expansion (could we enact the incident which caused her to be late?), but while it lasts it is riveting and for the same reason that watching any drama unfold is so compelling. Notice that the different role play exercises, essential to the content, can also be seen as a way of developing skill in drama. Its power derives from the fact that we are not just talking about events but we are watching them unfold before us in the present. The drama as recognised by numerous writers creates an 'eternal present' (Esslin 1987: 25).

Donaldson (1992) provides implicit theoretical underpinning for the appeal of drama. She has given an analysis of the way the mind develops by distinguishing four main modes of mental functioning: 'point', 'line', 'core construct' and 'transcendent'. They are defined by what she describes as 'loci of concern': the infant is more concerned with the 'here and now', with subsequent shifts in the level of generality of concern with increasing maturity. The first of these, the 'point mode', is the only one available to the young infant where the focus is always on the present moment. These developments come in succession as the child grows older but they do not replace one another. Drama could be said, in part, to operate within the 'point mode' and thus echoes our primary means of operating in the world. It is defined as 'a way of functioning in which the locus of concern is the directly experienced chunk of space-time that one currently inhabits: the here and now' (Esslin 1987: 3). Drama of course is never only concerned with the present for as Langer (1953: 307) has written 'it is only a present filled with its own future that is really dramatic'; it is clearly not confined to the point mode. However, whether one is participating in or observing drama it is the 'absorption in the moment' reminiscent of our first mental functioning as infants which gives it its particular potency as an art form and as a method of education. It is important to recognise a distinction between 'drama as art' and 'dramatic playing' as identified in the introduction to this book, but it is also important to acknowledge the close association of play and drama.

It provides security for the exploration of ideas

Drama is particularly valuable for introducing topics in subjects because of the concrete way it functions. As a way into an exploration of environmental issues a class have been asked to take the role of residents who are attending a public meeting to discuss the proposal to build a bypass. Because they will be in role the teacher is able to give them a 'script' which gives them in a sentence the point of view they will express at the meeting ('you are very much in favour of the bypass') and the real reason for their opinion ('it will bring more custom to your business') which may or may not accord with the reason the character is prepared to voice in public (a reluctance to see damage done to the local countryside).

It is the potential discrepancy between public voice and private opinion which will elevate the meeting above a simple discussion in role and will provide the underlying tension that 'things are not necessarily all that they seem'. The fact that pupils have been asked to adopt a point of view rather than present their own opinions provides greater security. Freed from ownership of the opinions they will express they can 'play' with the ideas in a creative and exploratory way.

Participating in drama is often seen to be a potentially embarrassing experience and it is important not to underestimate the exposure which participants can feel even at a young age when asked to engage in such activities. However, if sensitively handled the drama can also serve as a form of protection in which social roles and ideas can be explored within the safety of the 'mask'. A description of a lesson from the Kingman report (DES 1988: 45) provides another example of the way drama can offer protection. The context is an oral lesson in which individual pupils are report- ing back on group discussions based on whether the rights of individuals are threatened by establishing no-smoking areas. Each 'performance' is subject to com- ment by the other pupils on presentation and content. This lesson represents the Kingman ideal in which there is due emphasis on explicit attention to language within a 'language in use model'. However, there is a very interesting observation in the account which acknowledges that 'This teacher was aware that some members of the class found the format . . . too stressful.' That is not surprising because it can be very threatening to have one's own utterances challenged and criticised. The problem here is how to provide comment and feedback to the pupils which is not counter-productive. Imagine that the same lesson was set up as a drama about the creation of a television programme about no smoking areas. There is now the protec- tion of the role ('you may feel nervous if this is your first time in front of the camera'), the legitimisation of direction and comments, the chance to practise (let's have a run through before filming), the chance to comment on language and deliv- ery within a fictitious context which does not represent so much of a personal threat.

Drama works through focus and selection

In another classroom the class have been set the task in groups to prepare and pres- ent a modern dramatised version of the parable of the Good Samaritan. It is easy to see why such a task might be unsuccessful because many groups would be inclined to enact the narrative of the parable (including the violent attack by the robbers) and end up with the drama in chaos or dissolving into a humorous skit as a means of masking their lack of success. For the drama to succeed as drama the narrative must be transposed into 'plot' and to do this the groups will need to have a sense of dra- matic form and an ability to shape the work. This will entail being able to find a dramatic focus which at the same time will draw on their understanding of the sig- nificance of the parable. A group who has been taught drama effectively might recognise that there is no real need to enact the attack but realise that the focus and tension in the work might be derived from showing the pressure on the Samaritan figure by his peers not to offer assistance to the victim. It is difficult to envisage a successful enactment in dramatic terms which does not illuminate the pupils' understanding of the parable. A drama on the prodigal son would not necessarily have to show the son's travels or depict him eating with swine, but might focus on the brother's reluctance to join in the celebrations on his return home.

These examples illustrate that even in very simple cases the successful use of drama within subjects as so-called method does not differ in essence from the teaching of drama as subject, even though the emphasis in each case will be different: both require understanding of dramatic form and attention to content. That does not mean that drama as methodology should be promoted indiscriminately in schools. There is an argument for suggesting that this is a role for a drama specialist team-teaching with the subject teacher. Teachers who want to use drama as methodology need to understand the nature of drama as an art form or they will simply resort to telling pupils to get into groups and make up a play. Whether we wish to apply the term 'drama as learning' to drama as subject as well as method has to do with what we mean by this particular term.

Drama and learning

The concept of 'drama as a learning medium' can be a source of much confusion. It is easy to interpret the phrase as referring to the use of drama across the curriculum to teach other subjects. Traditionally, however, it has had a much broader usage referring rather to the whole tradition of drama embodied in the notion of 'drama in education'.

The confusion about drama as learning derives in part from the nature of the concept of learning itself. There is a usage of the term which embraces the widest notion of human development. Bruner (1971: 13) has commented that 'learning is so deeply ingrained in man that it is almost involuntary' and goes on to refer to the idea of education as a 'human invention that takes a learner beyond "mere" learning'. In one sense then it is possible to describe the most basic of human attributes as having been learned, and if drama facilitates the acquisition of these attributes in any way it is not wrong (although it may not be very helpful) to say that learning has taken place. Thus it is possible to apply the notion of learning to dramatic playing, improvisation, watching a play, even engaging in exercises and games. 'Learning' in that sense is not easily distinguished from 'development'.

This attempt to demarcate 'learning' from 'development' had parallels in writing in philosophy of education where some writers were arguing that to use learning in the context of education demanded that one be able to define both the particular object of learning and to recognise the intention of the learner as being of a distinctive kind. Put in very simple terms one is learning throughout one's life in the sense that one is developing, but for the term 'learning' to have any real purchase in an educational context it needs to be defined in specific ways. It seems obvious now to recognise that language forces us once more into a false dichotomy and an artificially narrow range of choices between 'development' and 'learning'; the reality is more complex. But the consequence has been that by applying the term 'learning' to drama, exponents made themselves vulnerable to the challenge that they should be able to say what that learning entails and critics have been quick to point out how vague and unsatisfactory such attempts have been.

An exploration of the way language relates to reality can contribute to our understanding of the particular power that drama has as a form of learning without feeling the need always to specify what new forms of learning arise as a result of the drama. The key concept here is 'expression' – not the notion of self-expression which was central to progressive theories of the 1960s but the idea of expression as a public, communal act. As Taylor (1980) has pointed out, traditional epistemology has privileged knowledge as a property of the individual and sees the process of communication as involving the transmission of those individual states of knowledge and belief. In contrast, expressive theories recognise that language serves not so much to externalise our internal thoughts and ideas but to build 'public space' between people, it serves to place certain matters in the public domain. That process is one of formulation and hence of transformation. 'Through language we can bring to explicit awareness what we formerly had only an implicit sense of. Through formulating some matter we bring it to fuller and clearer conscious' (ibid.: 262). In successful drama the same process of bringing about explicit awareness and making discriminations which are fundamental to human concerns is happening but far more intensely because the art form serves to select, focus and heighten the feeling content. In the past, exponents of drama in education have been aware of having created a successful drama with a group but have been unable to articulate in precise terms the learning which has taken place. An analysis which emphasises the process of articulation and expression as a form of learning makes sense of this dilemma. More importantly it forges a closer relationship between the role play which is going on in the history lesson, the drama workshop in the studio and the staging of a play in the theatre.

That does not mean that specific new insights, new learning, new transformations do not take place as a result of drama. After watching *King Lear* I may be prompted to say that I have learned something concrete about family relationships but the failure to articulate my learning in that way is not to deny the power and efficacy of the particular experience. The view of learning in drama which emphasises expression as the key concept also allows us to place the focus for evaluation not on what the participants have learned nor simply on the process of communication but on the quality of the articulacy in the dramatic form. The relationship between content and form is vital.

There will also be times when it is appropriate to attempt to capture the learning or understanding which arises as a result of drama in propositional form. Some writers have argued that to describe learning in this way is to deny the nature of the art form. But that is also to take a mistaken view of the way language has meaning. By formulating a proposition, for example, the pupils have learned that 'people are often prone to self-deception when making moral decisions' (an example from the Pied Piper project in Chapter 1), we are not saying that now pupils would be able to answer questions on a test about human behaviour, that they would be able to articulate their learning in this way, that before the lesson they had no inkling of this insight at all or indeed that this is all they have learned. The proposition captures more the 'flavour' of their learning. We only have to look to normal language use to see the force of this view. If someone tells us that an experience has made us learn that 'people can be very cruel' only the very crude or literal minded would say 'but surely you knew that already'. Learning and understanding is not an 'all or nothing' affair, although language sometimes makes us assume that such is the case.

Thus all successful drama is ultimately about learning and understanding in that as an art form it helps us to make sense of being in the world.

Drama and language development

The importance of drama for language development has been asserted by a number of authors and is fairly obvious because drama provides a variety of different contexts for language use. Thus if we ask pupils to take the roles of politicians, kings, teachers or priests the language demands will change accordingly. Language is often elevated in drama to suit the particular fictitious context. Notice how the language of the four-year-old in the following extract is formulated in complete sentences as he takes the role of doctor (the full twenty-minute transcript is given in Appendix A):

CHILD (as doctor): You have to have an injection. Don't cry. Don't cry. Don't shut your mouth. We have to put a bandage on it. (*Pause*) There it's finished. Will you ask your mummy to put a plaster on it when you get home please? Okay. Go on then. Tell your mummy to put a plaster on it, okay.

Elam (1980) has described the ways in which dramatic and everyday discourse differ, with the latter tending to be less neatly segmented, with false starts and repetitions and with more attention to 'phatic' communication – verbal exchanges which serve more to establish relationships rather than the communication of ideas.

The degree to which standard forms are used in the extract is significant. It is a reasonable objective that pupils should extend the linguistic registers at their disposal. One of the few effective ways to teach standard spoken English is in a drama context. Language is so much part of one's social and cultural identity that direct criticism of the way one speaks can feel like an attack on one's very being. Any attempt to impose standard English is likely to produce exactly the opposite of the desired result. Drama is able to provide contexts which both extend pupils' use of language and, because of the fictitious situation, protect them from feelings of linguistic inadequacy. This is as much true for reading and writing as it is for speaking and listening.

However, the full value of drama for the development of language can only be appreciated in relation to an understanding of the power of the art form in creating contexts embedded with feeling, meaning and motivation and in bracketing experiences. In *Children's Minds* Donaldson (1978) challenged many of Piaget's assumptions about the intellectual capacity of young children by repeating his experiments in ways which could be described as using a dramatic format.

Thus an abstract problem about trying to discern what a person would see from another position became easier when it was reframed as a problem about a naughty boy hiding from a policeman. A problem of continuity which asked whether the number of objects in a row increased when they were spaced out more became easier when a naughty teddy came to interfere with the spacing of the objects rather than the experimenter. Donaldson's conclusion was that the language of the experimenter and the task itself are much more difficult for the child if they are removed from familiar human feelings, purposes and goals.

The implications for education are important because much of the language that is used in education remains alien to the more natural way language is employed spontaneously by children. Donaldson describes how children when observed in play showed an ability to make logical inferences which they did not show when tested. She argues that schools often do not realise the difficulties involved for pupils in moving from a use of language which takes place in what she calls 'real-life' situations to a more remote context which reflects the more abstract nature of the thought processes. She suggests that a clearer understanding of what is involved in making that move in new disembedded modes is necessary in education. The importance of drama is that it extends the sphere of reference outside the familiar events of the child's life, but the language and thinking which is employed is embedded in the sense that due attention is given to feeling, intention and motivation.

But it is in the nature of drama as an art form to move, so to speak, in two directions at once. It brings us closer to 'real' experiences because it engages us in human, fictitious contexts but at the same time it distances us from the equivalent real experience because it selectively brackets extraneous factors. In the exchange between doctor and mother, the four-year-old is able to enter the territory of death and burial precisely because there is no pressure to use language in a real context.

CHILD (as doctor): We'll just have to get him buried. There's nothing the nurse can do about it.
ADULT (as mother): Well, how do you do that? What do you mean bury him?
CHILD (as doctor): We put a cross up. I've got a cross in my doctor's house here. We have to put a cross and put his name. What's his name?
ADULT (as mother): His name is David.
CHILD (as doctor): So we have to put David, okay. Come on, we just have to bury him.

Real communication, particularly in public contexts with strangers, may be full of subtexts, innuendo and self-consciousness which can become under more conscious control in drama. A leader in real life may be unaware that she is causing all sorts of misunderstandings, envy, rivalry and offence. In drama the consequences of what one says can be determined before, during or after the event. Drama helps us not just to use language but to experience our use of language and to recognise that only fairly trivial uses of language are transparent.

Drama policies

The role of drama within a school and within the National Curriculum is then likely to be complex, able to fulfil different educational aims in different contexts. A school policy would help bring coherence of drama provision within individual schools.

It is easy to become cynical about policy statements for they can often mean that the responsibility for the particular issue (e.g. equal opportunities or health and safety) is thought to have been discharged simply by the production of a written document. However, there are clear reasons why a policy on drama provision within a school is necessary. As suggested earlier the relationship between English and drama at secondary level needs to be established, if the latter is taught as a separate subject. For example, it needs to be decided which department has responsibility for teaching Shakespeare and what degree of collaboration is possible. Visits to the theatre can be seen as part of broad policy on drama and can be usefully coordinated. At primary level, where drama is more easily used as a starting point or central focus for topic work, a policy is needed on the degree to which drama is also timetabled as a separate subject. It should be recognised that not all staff within a school will be able to employ drama methods successfully and there is a strong case for specialist provision.

Possibilities for integration with other subjects on the curriculum need to be identified as does the potential for team teaching. School productions need to be seen not as something totally separate but part of the broad drama provision within a school. A coordinated policy for drama will above all help other staff understand its particular value as an art form in its own right and as a teaching method, and will help establish drama as a potent force in a school.

Here then is an indication of some of the likely content of a school drama policy:

- statement of broad aims of drama as both arts subject and teaching method
- explanation of curriculum provision and specialist staff
- summary of programmes of study and schemes of work for drama
- policy assessment and evaluation

- statement about drama resources
- special needs and equal opportunities
- relationship between drama and other subjects – possibilities for integration
- relationship of drama to areas such as citizenship and PSHE.
- policy on visits to theatre, visits to school by theatre groups and productions
- (at secondary level) provision for examinations.

A whole-school policy in a school will provide an appropriate basis for the planning of individual lessons and schemes of work, the subject of the next chapter.

Further reading

The Secondary Drama Teacher's Handbook published by National Drama has a section on drama's place in the curriculum (as well as guidance on a wide range of other topics including writing a drama policy). See also Somers (1994) *Drama in the Curriculum*. Publications showing how drama can be linked with the Literacy Strategy include Winston, J. (2000) *Drama, Literacy and Moral Education 5–11*, Ackroyd, J. (2000) *Literacy Alive*, Toye, N. and Prendiville, F. (2000) *Drama and Traditional Story for the Early Years*, Baldwin, P. and Fleming, K. (2003) *Teaching Literacy Through Drama*. The Secondary Head's Association (1998) publication *Drama Sets You Free!* argues for the place of drama in schools. Descriptions of the way drama can be used to develop language can be found in Byron, K. (1986) *Drama in the English Classroom*, Neelands, J. (1992) *Learning Through Imagined Experience*. Publications which deal specifically with drama and the National Curriculum in the primary school include Clipson-Boyles, S. (1998) *Drama in Primary English Teaching*, Baldwin, P. (1991) *Stimulating Drama*, Kitson, N. and Spiby, I. (1997) *Primary Drama Handbook*, Winston, J. (2000) *Drama, Literacy and Moral Education 5–11*.

3

Planning for drama: lessons and schemes of work

Planning

CHAPTER 1 described different approaches to teaching drama based on the Pied Piper story. One simple activity involved the pupils in pairs in a supermarket or other modern context gradually discovering that they both have rats. What is the purpose of an activity of that kind? To teach them how to role play? To encourage cooperation? To prepare them to react if an infestation of rats happens in later life? To understand something about social pressure? To develop their language? To understand how dramatic dialogue can be created by withholding information? This chapter will address the various problems associated with planning specific lessons and schemes of work in which questions of purpose play a key part.

At first it might appear that this would simply be a question of offering a broad framework, examples of specific lesson plans and a warning that the best laid plans can easily come unstuck. However, it is not that straightforward. Any framework is likely to carry assumptions about learning and the nature of drama. Planning, which seems to be above all a very practical matter, actually gives rise to a number of theoretical considerations and faces teachers with questions of priority and value. For example, the decision whether to operate with a highly structured lesson plan which leaves little room for pupils to determine the shape and content of the lesson or to go for more flexibility is a decision which does not just depend on the experience and security of the teacher but has to do with fundamental beliefs about how people learn. On the other hand, it is of little value if ideological and theoretical perspectives override practical considerations if the result in the classroom is not productive. To put it in concrete terms, there is little point in the teacher, motivated by a theoretical perspective drawn from particular learning theories, starting the lesson in a very open-ended way if the result in the classroom is chaos. Effective planning for drama needs to balance theoretical and pragmatic considerations.

As with other chapter titles in this book, the idea of 'planning for drama' contains ambiguities. Is the emphasis on planning for successful drama or on planning the learning which comes about as a result of the drama, and to what extent can these objectives be conceived separately? Is it the teacher's task to plan drama or should the aim be for pupils to acquire that ability? A major challenge in setting objectives is whether these should relate to the development of specific drama skills (learning in drama) or whether they should relate to the learning which comes about as a result of the drama (learning through drama). To emphasise skills at the expense of content runs the risk of promoting busy activity without any meaningful purpose, but to phrase objectives in terms of learning content alone is to diminish the potential for subject-specific assessment and progression.

It is important not to adopt any one planning framework without considering the implied assumptions about drama and learning. This need for caution in adopting a particular planning model applies whether drama is being taught as a separate subject or not. It was argued in the previous chapter that there is far more in common between drama as 'subject' and as 'method' than is often thought and most of the considerations which will be discussed in this chapter apply to both. The aims are likely to vary, but such practical considerations as anticipating pitfalls, taking account of the available space and questions of discipline are all relevant no matter what form the drama takes. It is also important to consider the relationship between a single lesson or project and an entire scheme of work.

Having received some rather derisory treatment in much educational literature in the 1970s, objectives are back with a vengeance. Clear objectives are now seen almost universally as the key to successful teaching and learning. A common model for curriculum and lesson planning involves the identification of clear objectives, the choice of teaching activities which will fulfil those objectives, followed by testing of some sort to determine whether they have been fulfilled. The logic and simplicity of the model may be compelling until one realises that inevitably it ignores much that is important in teaching and learning contexts. It implies, for example, that the means (the teaching activity) can easily be separated from the ends (the objectives). It was seen in the previous chapter how the decision to use drama as a method can often expand and deepen the learning; it is not just a simple matter, for example, of arbitrarily choosing between using drama and showing a video. The model also implies that the only worthwhile objectives are those which can easily be identified in advance of the teaching activity, and denies the important contribution made by the learner in determining the object of learning; this is a particularly important consideration in arts subjects when often the most worthwhile outcomes are difficult to specify in advance. An objectives-led model implies that the only worthwhile objectives are those which are easily assessed and is based on the assumption that language is always 'transparent', that everyone will share a common understanding of the learning outcomes simply because these are written out and shared in advance.

Language is often ambiguous and open to interpretation. Much of the difficulty associated with criterion-referenced testing derives from such difficulties. Even if we take the simplest of objectives in mathematics, the ability to add two numbers, it is not clear exactly what it means to say that pupils have acquired that ability. For some pupils the accurate performance of the task may depend on whether the numbers are written in a linear sequence (25 + 32 =) or whether one number is written above the other. It is little wonder therefore that there is research which has established that instead of following the objectives-first model, many teachers approach planning by choosing activities which they think will be successful. 'They select from conveniently available sources, such as teacher editions of textbooks or curriculum guides, those activities they believe will engage student attentions' (Sardo-Brown 1990: 58). I suspect many teachers in drama operate in practice on the basis of choosing what will 'work' at the same time perhaps feeling guilty in the current educational climate about the apparent lack of objectivity and accountability implied in that notion. However, it helps to unpack what is meant by choosing an idea which 'works'. In the context of a lesson aimed at creating drama it is a shorthand way of saying that the end result has been successful, that there has been emotional engagement appropriate to the topic, that there has been sufficient tension and focus in the work. We could go on to say that if the drama has been successful the pupils are likely to have enhanced their understanding both of drama and of the subject matter.

As with so many issues in drama teaching it is easy to be torn between two extremes. On the one hand, there is the appeal of an objectives-first model which appears to fulfil criteria of accountability and objectivity but the logic of which distorts and reduces the richness of the education process it purports to describe. On the other hand, an approach which is unable to specify anything concrete on the grounds that this is necessarily a simplification of the process is hardly acceptable. There is a tendency in drama to deny that it is possible to talk about learning objectives because that distorts the nature of drama as art. But the choice is not that stark. If one recognises that all language and theorising is necessarily reductive and a simplification, and indeed that is its value, then the way is paved for taking a more reasonable (as opposed to rational) approach to planning.

The distinction between what is 'reasonable' and 'rational' is very helpful here. It is interesting that the notion of 'rational planning' came to have somewhat negative connotations implying as it did a sacrifice of human complexity for a reductive logic. A 'reasonable' approach to planning would recognise that teachers (as well as parents and pupils) need to know what particular activities are aiming to achieve and would acknowledge that broad aims are essential in giving long-term direction to the work. It would also acknowledge that the formulation of objectives need not serve to circumscribe learning outcomes.

So much for the argument which urges caution in the use of objectives. However, it is also necessary to recognise their value in giving focus and direction to teaching. An examination of lesson plans published in books or on the Internet reveals that many writers on drama do not find the specification of objectives easy.

They are often written in vague terms as in the following examples drawn from a variety of published plans:

- work in groups
- use imagination
- take on a role
- develop improvisational skills
- explore the use of space
- respond to teacher in role
- work together as a pair.

Objectives of this kind often do not give enough focus and direction to a lesson. Some are more related to social skills (ability to work in groups) or very general aptitude (use imagination). That is not to say that increasing social skills is not a clear benefit of drama but as a lesson objective it is very vague and general. Without more focused objectives a lesson can easily consist of a series of arbitrary activities (warm-ups, games, pairs exercises, still images) without an overall sense of purpose.

Another type of lesson objective found in the literature relates to learning content, e.g. understand why people are forced to leave their homes. There is an argument for expressing the purpose of a lesson in this way because it underlines the importance of content. However, to try to express such outcomes as objectives (as opposed to just the theme of the lesson or project) runs the risk of actually limiting the pupils' exploration of the content. Objectives of this kind moreover are not easy to assess.

Whether in the context of drama as a separate subject or in English it makes sense therefore to make the objectives related to the specific drama focus. At various times in its history a range of broad aims for drama have been advanced, such as personal growth, learning and understanding, and the acquisition of skills in drama. In practice these are all to some extent likely to be outcomes of successful drama. It is helpful, however, to distinguish between the *value* of an activity and the *aims* of the teacher as intentional agent. Thus the development of personal qualities such as confidence and sociability may be valuable outcomes of the drama but they would not necessarily relate directly to the teacher as intentional agent. It makes more sense to see the objectives in terms of development of ability in drama. As long as these are treated with some flexibility and not too mechanistically, they can help give depth to the content rather than detract from it. As suggested above, it is important to guard against a reductive approach to teaching drama which promotes mindless activity without due attention to content. It is for this reason that a balanced lesson plan is likely to be achieved by specifying objectives as well as the content area. This avoids having to describe learning in relation to content in propositional terms (the problems with this were described in Chapter 2).

Thus an objective such as: *understand different ways of beginning drama* might relate to such a content focus as: *exploration of individual and social responsibilities towards the old*. Notice how the content focus is more open-ended and does not resort to specifying and circumscribing learning outcomes which would run counter to the true spirit of artistic endeavour. A more circumscribed learning objective with regard to content might result in a sentimental drama about being nice to the old instead of exploring genuine human concerns and conflicts which can arise in families. This chapter opened with an example drawn from the Pied Piper project. It can now be seen that the drama-specific object 'To understand how dramatic dialogue can be created by withholding information' relates specifically to the thematic content related to social pressure.

Table 3.1 below gives examples of more focused objectives and related drama activities.

TABLE 3.1 Examples of specific drama objectives and their related activites

Objective	Related drama activity
Use space in order to create different moods (hostility, relaxation, nervousness).	Creation of different tableaux in one location (doctor's waiting room, train carriage).
Understand differences between narrative and plot.	Groups given outline of a story and asked to sequence the drama in different ways.
Use non-naturalistic techniques to create dramatic effect.	Creation of group improvisations in which one character pauses to address the audience.
Understand how incongruity and withholding identity can be used for comic effect.	In pairs, a counsellor or police detective conducts an interview with a character from a fairy-tale.
Use music to enhance mood.	Groups are asked to select two contrasting pieces of music to accompany a mime on theme of leaving home.
Deepen characters by exploring background information and motivation.	Hotseating characters from a play.

Not all lessons introduce a new drama focus, and lessons take different forms and have different purposes (introductory lessons, continuation lessons). The specification of new learning outcomes is not always appropriate for every lesson. Often the objectives will need to be written in a way which acknowledges this, e.g. 'to consolidate X' or 'to continue to develop skills in X'. As suggested earlier it would be a mistake to assume that there is only one, correct way to set out a lesson plan. However, the example given in Figure 3.1 shows one way of doing so for the Pied Piper lesson described at the start of this chapter.

Pied Piper Lesson Plan

Objectives:

- To understand how dramatic dialogue can be created by withholding information
- To further develop skills in pairs role play and script writing

Content focus: the way in which social pressure affects people's behaviour

Resources:

- Copies of Pied Piper poem from last week
- Paper/pens

Lesson sequence

Introduction

Warm-up game: 'Sculptures' (One person takes up a position in centre of circle another completes the picture. A third person taps the first on the shoulder and creates another picture with the second and so on.)

Recap by recreating tableaux from last week's lesson while teacher reads out relevant extracts from poem.

Pairs improvisation: pupils in pairs as neighbours. They both suspect they have rats – they have not actually seen a rat but they have seen signs. They meet and both discover that they have the same suspicions. Improvisation to last only a very short period of time as pupils will not be able to sustain for very long.

Repeat the exercise – this time at a signal from the teacher the pairs meet with another pair. At another signal the fours become eight representing the spread of gossip and consternation in the town.

Group discussion: How could we extend the first pairs activity? Why might the neighbours be reluctant to admit their fears? How could this be represented?

Demonstration – teacher and volunteer: this time rats are not mentioned but an audience who knows the situation might be able to pick up clues that the neighbours are uneasy about something.

Pairs work to develop the improvisations and then script.

Presentation of work: class identify techniques which different pairs used to withhold the key information. Is this the way people behave? Are all people like that?

Assessment opportunities: final presentation will give an indication of whether they have understood and are able to include the key ingredient.

Evaluation: . . .

FIGURE 3.1   Example lesson plan

Planning schemes of work

The same tension between working within a secure structure while at the same time preserving enough flexibility applies to writing schemes of work as well as planning lessons. Schemes of work are often seen just as collections of ideas and resources as opposed to lesson plans which deal with the real business of structuring learning. However, it is important to give thought to the shape of a scheme of work because this will reflect the way in which progression (a topic which will be examined in Chapter 9) is conceived. Long-term plans will reflect the broad schemes of work for an entire key stage broken down into units of work (lasting, for example, a half term each). Medium-term plans will indicate the broad approach within each unit without the detail which belongs to lesson plans. The further reading section at the end of this chapter gives details of publications containing examples of schemes of work.

When planning schemes of work in the context of English the content is likely to be determined by the National Curriculum or Literacy Strategy with drama illuminating the novels, poems, writing, speaking and listening tasks. Otherwise, planning schemes of work can be undertaken in different ways, in terms of theme, project, script, genres and styles, or skills (see Table 3.2). A thematic approach has tended to be more closely associated with models of drama where the emphasis was very much on the content of the drama (bullying, school, family conflicts). One advantage of this approach to planning is that it is more engaging and exciting for the pupils to see their drama in terms of 'murder at the disco' or 'life in the city' than 'non-naturalistic techniques'. A purely text-based approach provides both a clear focus for the drama and a more tangible indication of what the work is about but may marginalise some pupils and bore others (depending of course on the specific approach in the classroom).

The term 'project' is being used here as an umbrella term to refer to specific work which extends over a period of time but is not specifically related to a theme (theatre in education project or the devising of a pantomime for performance). An approach based on genres or dramatic forms might also include topics such as theatre in education but also physical theatre or theatre of the absurd. A skills focus speaks for itself; setting objectives will be straightforward but it runs the risk of isolating skills from content. In practice it is probably a good idea to plan schemes of work using a variety of these methods. For example, a long-term scheme might usefully begin with a thematic approach to engage the pupils' interest and include work on a specific text at a later stage. The scheme might culminate in a project, e.g. a piece of theatre in education at a local junior school.

TABLE 3.2 Approaches to planning schemes of work

Planning approach	Comment
Thematic (e.g. the environment, pirates, space travel).	It is clearly pupil-centred and places emphasis on meaning. It relates more to personal growth aims. Emphasis is often on creating rather than responding. It is difficult for pupils to chart progression in terms of content so the drama focus needs to be described.
Project (e.g. theatre in education, researching and devising a play for performance, work based on other subjects).	A 'project' approach is often useful at the end of a year as it involves more focus on product and celebration of achievement. The fact that it has a clear, concrete goal is a useful motivator.
Text-based (either play texts or scripts written by pupils).	The advantage of working from a text is that the focus is clear and this can take pressure away from the teacher to keep coming up with fresh content. It is also easier to link with the English syllabus. The text project can of course include 'process work' – improvisation, conventions, whole-group drama.
Genres and styles (e.g. melodrama, masks).	This approach brings more breadth to the drama syllabus and makes the subject knowledge content more specific. Unless approached in the right way, it may be difficult for pupils to engage.
Skills.	Objectives are clear and planning for assessment is therefore more straightforward. There is of course the risk of marginalising any significant content unless approached in an appropriate way.

The scheme of work can only be properly planned in context. It is a good idea to pay considerable attention to the beginning of the scheme in order to engage the pupils' interest. It is also sensible to structure the work fairly closely in the early stages allowing more flexibility as the work takes on a momentum of its own. The following questions will bring structure to the scheme:

- What are the broad aims (related to both the drama focus and content)?
- What is the range of attainment in the class?
- How much time is available – number and duration of lessons?
- How does the scheme relate to the pupils' prior learning?
- What are the assessment strategies?

As suggested above, when drama does not exist as a separate subject the schemes of work are likely to be linked more closely to the English National Curriculum and Literacy Strategy. Examples of the way the topics might be structured for a medium-term outline plan at Key Stage 2 are given in Table 3.3 (The full project was trialled with a Year 5 class and is written up in Chaplin 1999.)

TABLE 3.3 Medium-term outline plan – Irish Potato Famine

Session theme	Resources	Drama activities	Related work
Introducing the topic.	Picture of a family outside their hut at the time of the famine.	Freeze frame. Question teacher in role as one of the family members.	Drawing map of Ireland. Researching the date 1841.
Discovering the potato blight.	Information sheet about possible causes of the blight.	Exercise – spreading gossip. Pairs role play (calling on a neighbour) after demonstration by teacher.	List different reasons for crop failing. Letter to relative in England about the crop failure.
Evictions and soup kitchens.	Facsimile document from the time about the closing of soup kitchens. Eye-witness accounts of evictions.	Thought tracking related to eviction. Freeze frame. Small-group work.	Creation of a soup kitchen poster. Eye-witness account of an eviction.
The workhouse.	Paper and pens. Example of script.	Whole-class improvisation – committee meeting. Script work.	Written account of the committee recommendations. Drawing up the workhouse rules.
Emigration.	List of examples of conflicting statements made by those thinking about emigration.	Voices in the head – characters' thoughts as they decide whether to emigrate.	Diary in role of an emigrant.
Final presentation.	Sheet with narrative outline. Various props.	Small-group presentations.	Final reflective piece on the project as a whole.

It is important that the two important aims which will be a function of the teacher's planning – the development of ability in drama and understanding of content – can be given due recognition in planning and kept in constant dialogue and balance when teaching. Any significant understanding of what being 'good at drama' entails must include reference to content. In the following discussion of pitfalls and considerations in planning drama these two aspects will be kept in mind.

Common pitfalls

Emphasis on narrative rather than plot

One of the most common mistakes both teachers and pupils make when planning drama is to think in terms of 'narrative' (the basic outline of the story) rather than 'plot' (the means by which the narrative events are structured). An attempt to plan drama with insufficient awareness of the constraints of the form in which one is working will often result in the elaboration of a complex story followed by an attempt to translate that action into drama with disappointing results. I can recall watching a small group of Year 8 pupils as explorers on an island attempt to enact their complex adventures which included the unearthing of buried treasure, the discovery of a lost tribe, the search for an antidote for a mysterious illness, all of which was woven into a coherent and intricate story. Despite their considerable motivation to succeed (in no sense were they using the lesson to have a riotous time) they were unable to sustain the drama successfully. The tendency to think in terms of complex narrative is enhanced by the fact that pupils' experience of drama is often drawn from film and television with its capacity to change location easily and accelerate the action. The pupils here needed to be given a specific, narrower focus for the group work – for example, they are on an island and find some inconclusive evidence which suggests that they may not be alone. It is interesting to note that the drama which is more likely to work as drama has more potential for exploration of the content (what sort of signs would an indigenous people leave? Are these people likely to be hostile? Is it our moral duty as scientists to go on and explore or should we depart now and leave them undisturbed?). The difference between 'narrative' and 'plot' needs to be explored specifically with pupils.

The problem with the latter suggestion is that teachers new to drama often have the same misconceptions. I watched a group planning a lesson on the theme of a journey to another planet using whole-group improvisation. They had decided that the pupils would be space travellers to another planet who would discover a 'Brave New World' society based on a rigid class system and would have to face a decision whether to offer assistance to the rebels who were mounting a challenge to the government. The details were in fact rather more complex but the important point is that although there was no lack of potential for both excitement and moral decision-making, very little thought had been given to how the drama would be realised (e.g. begin with pairs meeting between a rebel and traveller). However, this example embodies another 'mistake', which is to assume that the particular class will share the same enthusiasm for the chosen topic of space travel.

Failure to engage pupils with the content

The example above placed too much emphasis on content without sufficient attention to the demands of the dramatic form. It is also possible to pay insufficient attention to the nature of the content. For drama to succeed, motivation needs to be high. Fortunately, as discussed in the previous chapter, pupils do tend to enjoy participation in drama if they are helped to succeed and protected from embarrassment and exposure. When drama is drawing on other curriculum subjects, the problem of motivation with respect to the content is less likely to be a problem. However, when choosing content other than scripted text, the choice often seems fairly arbitrary.

Why, for example, should a class necessarily all be interested in the chosen topic? This a key issue in planning schemes of work and reinforces the need for variety. A 'project' approach at some stage in the year can give pupils choice of subject matter. The importance of pupils being involved from the start explains why it was very common in the early days of drama in education to start the lesson by asking the pupils to make suggestions and vote on the topic for the drama. This approach has the obvious advantage of involving the pupils, but because the advance planning can extend no further than posing the question 'what shall we do a play about?' it carries the obvious risk of the teacher not knowing how to proceed once the pupils have chosen their topic. It is a tall order for the teacher to be able to see the educational potential in their choice of topic and initiate the drama in a way which helps the pupils to create successful work. The very open start is not one which occurs very often these days but, as suggested, there are ways of giving pupils some choice of content. The recipe for a successful drama may be a very secure framework which gives the teacher confidence but which gives pupils enough freedom to make choices within that structure.

Some balance then needs to be found between starting the lesson in a very open-ended way and plunging the pupils into a particular topic for which they have no strong motivation. There are a number of solutions. Just as drama can be used as a 'way in' to a particular topic in history or a novel in English, it is sometimes necessary to think carefully about how the topic for drama will be introduced. It is not a question of manipulating the pupils to choose the particular topic the teacher had intended (although it may look like that) but of recognising that a large group of individuals may need to be drawn into a topic gradually. Alternative starting points useful for introducing the subject matter of the drama (e.g. the use of artefacts, pictures, headlines, script) are useful and will be discussed in Chapter 9. The use of games and warm-ups which create a workshop atmosphere can also lead successfully into the chosen topic: suggestions will be given in Chapter 4.

A note of caution is needed on the practice of involving pupils in discussion before starting the drama, which is often recommended in the literature as a way of engaging them with the topic. It is often difficult for teacher and pupils to make the transition from talking about the drama to actually starting it. The advantage of preliminary talk is that it allows pupils to bring their own experiences to bear on the subject matter in hand, but the talk may actually lead them away from possibilities in drama. Take, for example, the subject matter of 'ghosts' or 'haunted houses'. Most classes will talk endlessly about this topic but their talk may take them into a narrative mode which creates a level of expectation that is difficult to fulfil. The appropriate approach in drama to avoid the descent into playing ghosts might be to take an oblique approach which puts the pupils in role as investigators or which explores the past events which caused the haunting.

However, these suggestions may well run counter to the pupils' expectations which are built up as they talk their way into the topic. In other words the drama would more successfully be built from a concrete, particular action within the drama rather than from outside – for example, in pairs conduct the interview with the person who claims to have seen a ghost but whose story is doubted by the interviewer.

Failure to plan questions and discussions

To the experienced teacher the suggestion that questions should be planned might indicate a form of rigidity and mechanism which is in danger of promoting poor teaching because it implies a lack of sensitivity to what has actually happened in the lesson. I have sympathy with that view. Nevertheless I have observed a number of projects collapse because when it came to the word 'discuss' in the lesson plan the teacher floundered in a rather vague fashion not knowing what to ask or how to proceed. This often happens after the presentation of group plays or tableaux when the word 'discuss' often translates into a rather vague question thrown to the class as a whole, such as 'what did you think of it?' When planning a drama it is well worth thinking through the possible questions which are likely to be productive in helping pupils respond to the drama – it does not mean that these have to be followed in slavish and mechanistic fashion.

Failure to plan how group work will be supported

I would suspect that some form of group preparation and presentation is likely to figure in a large number of drama projects and in my experience this is a common feature of the way drama tends to be used within other subjects. In subjects such as history, RE and English, pupils will be asked in groups to 'make up a play' often with such disappointing results that the teacher is reluctant to venture into drama again. I am likewise struck by the number of drama publications which make the assumption that pupils merely need to be told what it is they are expected to enact and they will do so effectively. It is at such moments in lessons when teachers tell groups to 'develop a scene showing how the inmates might disappear' or 'show the travellers leaving' that otherwise successful topics break down. The emphasis in drama in education on whole-class plays controlled by the teacher arose partly in recognition of the fact that pupils left to themselves will generally not produce successful drama. It is precisely for that reason that group work needs to be carefully introduced and pupils helped with such matters as how to slow down the action, how to deal with physical action, how to use pause effectively to create tension, how to use non-naturalistic techniques. More suggestions on group work will be given in Chapter 5.

Planning considerations

The available space

One of drama's essential distinguishing factors as an art form is that it takes place in real space and time. It is helpful therefore to think about the importance of space and the best way of using it. There are two considerations to be borne in mind: the space available for the lesson and the space which is created for the drama. Drama can take place anywhere even in the smallest of classrooms but there is little doubt that the range of work which is possible can be constrained by the available space. Drama in education has tended to place less emphasis on the degree to which external factors influence the quality of the work because of a reluctance to generate artificial and inauthentic responses – the use of lights and music has received less attention than the engagement of feeling through the content of the work. Drama is generated through the imaginative capacity of pupils to create symbolism and often it is the degree to which their reliance on external features in the environment is minimised which creates successful drama. However, it is also true that pupils may find it more difficult to believe in their classroom as a desert island than they would if they were in an atmospheric drama studio. The creation of 'mood' is an appropriate objective because it implies the use of external factors to contribute to the creation of an appropriate feeling. The absence of an ideal environment should not prevent much successful drama taking place in a school, but that fact should not stop teachers lobbying for a dedicated space for their work.

The ideal space for drama is a purpose-built studio which can be used both for workshops and for small performances. Very often it is assumed that the appropriate space for drama is a large main hall, indeed that is often the only available space apart from a classroom. Large open spaces are often associated with very active movement and may create the wrong type of atmosphere for drama. They can be vulnerable to interruption and may be full of nooks and crannies into which the drama can spill making control more difficult. By marking off an appropriate area, a more intimate atmosphere can be created as long as the boundaries are defined clearly with the class in advance. Often it is more suitable to work in the classroom than to go to the hall, in which case it is worth considering whether it is actually necessary to remove furniture or not. Such techniques as teacher in role, pairs improvisation, questioning in role (to be discussed in Chapter 5) can be comfortably employed in the classroom without disturbing the furniture.

The experience of the class

One of the advantages of a whole-school policy on drama recommended in Chapter 2 is that all teachers in a school are able to see their use of drama in the wider context in which drama is taught in the school. It has been part of the tradition of drama in education to place less emphasis on the ability of the individual or group in drama but more on the teacher or group leader. If the drama has not been successful the assumption tended to be not that the participants were not very good and did not perform the tasks well but that the leader did not facilitate the work properly. From a pedagogic point of view I think this tradition has been laudable and a welcome change from the opposite trend often found in other subjects of blaming pupils for the lack of success of a particular lesson. Classes who do not respond to discussion are often judged to be lacking in vitality or 'dead' instead of questioning the particular techniques being used.

The experience of the teacher

Some of the most powerful approaches to drama such as teacher in role and whole-group improvisation can be the most daunting. It is important that teachers are not put off using drama because of the prevalence of these techniques in the drama literature. It will hopefully be apparent from this book that much valuable drama work can be achieved by the teacher adopting more conventional teaching stances which feel less threatening. Thus a planned workshop which directs the pupils through warm-ups, pairs improvisation, small-group work on text, brief performances (of say three or four lines) can produce effective drama which will give the teacher confidence to experiment with more challenging personal involvement in the work.

The age and maturity of the group

It is not simply a matter of the age of pupils which is significant in planning drama; the degree of maturity and social cohesion which exists within a group needs to be taken into account. This is where preliminary warm-up exercises and games at the start of a drama programme can be useful in diagnosing attitudes and aptitudes, and giving practice in practical activities which are not too threatening or demanding. Group work may be inhibited simply by arguments in which case it may be advisable to alter one's approach to groupings next lesson.

Control

It is questionable whether much can be learned about classroom control from reading about it. Rules of thumb, such as learn pupils' names, use positive encouragement, do not make idle threats, do not be too friendly, be firm but fair, are sensible enough but they do not take into account the fact that how one behaves in a classroom is as much to do with how one feels at the time, one's personality and values, as it is to do with what one knows. I have not met any group of student teachers who have not been able to generate in a very short space of time virtually all the types of advice about discipline which can be found in the literature. That does not mean that they are necessarily able to function effectively yet in the classroom.

In the case of drama it is similarly possible to offer hints on control – e.g. in large spaces such as the hall establish which areas are out of bounds, employ a 'no physical contact' rule, form a circle or oval for discussion, have a specific signal which will always bring the class to order. However, rather than reduce discipline merely to a matter of rules it is perhaps more helpful to understand some of the tensions which arise because of the nature of the subject. Some of the behaviour problems which arise do so because of positive, overexuberant attitudes combined with poor lesson structures.

Further reading

For schemes of work at primary level see Winston, J. (2000) *Drama, Literacy and Moral Education 5–11*, Scrivens, L. (1994) *Drama in the Primary School*, Chaplin, A. (1999) *Drama 9–11*, Readman, G. and Lamont, G. (1994) *Drama – A Handbook for Primary Teachers*. For an example of a scheme of work for Key Stage 3 see Bennathan, J. (2000) *Developing Drama Skills*. For specific chapters on planning see Kempe, A. and Nicholson, H. (2001) *Learning to Teach Drama 11–18*, Kitson, N. and Spiby, I. (1997) *Primary Drama Handbook*, Owens, A. and Barber, K. (1997) *Dramaworks*, Bolton, G. (1992a) *New Perspectives on Classroom Drama*, Morgan, N. and Saxton, J. (1987) *Teaching Drama*. For planning approaches to 'process' drama see Taylor, P. (2000) *The Drama Classroom*, Bowell, P. and Heap, B.S. (2001) *Planning Process Drama*, O'Neill, C. (1995) *Drama Worlds*.

Starting drama

Common misconceptions

MANY STUDENTS AND TEACHERS embark on simple role play with a class only to come out shell-shocked and disillusioned. 'They started hitting each other and fighting . . . they just collapsed in giggles . . . I could not get them to take it seriously . . . they kept making cars out of chairs and pretending to drive around, screeching brakes . . .' Role play is used on all sorts of courses with adults often in ways guaranteed to alienate and embarrass the participants. Although the examples here will be drawn from lessons with pupils, the general suggestions for facilitating drama are relevant at all levels. For the purposes of this chapter I do not propose to wrestle with conceptual differences between 'role play', 'drama' and 'improvisation', interesting and important though those distinctions are. The contention here is that an understanding of the ingredients which create successful drama needs to feed into the most basic forms of work, including role play. There are certain steps teachers can take and considerations to be borne in mind which come automatically to the experienced drama teacher but which are not by any means obvious to the teacher who is new to the subject. The focus here then will be on pairs work in drama and the constructive use of games and warm-up exercises.

It is not the argument of this chapter that pairs work is necessarily always the best starting point for teachers and pupils who are new to drama; some of the conventions which will be described in Chapter 6, such as tableau or questioning in role, can provide a very secure and controlled beginning. However, while mime, movement and monologue are all important aspects of drama, it is dialogue which is at the centre of the 'dramatic web' (Szondi 1987: 17). An ability to facilitate pairs work effectively requires an understanding of the essential nature of dramatic activity which will feed into all other aspects of work whether drama is being taught as a separate subject or as method. It will also prevent some of the misunderstandings about how best to start drama with a class which, although mistaken, are often based on a sound rationale derived from experience of the theatre on the one hand and knowledge of children's capacity for dramatic play on the other. For experience of the theatre can lead to assumptions that in order to initiate drama one always needs to cast characters, plan a scenario and direct the action; it is an understanding of the way the theatre works at a deeper level which needs to inform the facilitation of drama. On the other hand, knowledge of children's capacity for dramatic play can lead to an underestimation of the degree of structure and teaching of specific drama techniques which is required. With the proviso that it is unwise to be too dogmatic because exceptions can always be found to disprove the rule, it is possible to discuss in more detail some mistaken assumptions about the best way to start drama.

Casting

A conventional play text normally begins with a list of 'dramatis personae' and it might be reasonable to assume that the appropriate way to begin drama, whether basing work on text or improvisation, is to distribute parts. However, in the case of work with play texts, launching into the acting of a part demands a considerable degree of skill and experience. (Alternative ways of starting work with texts will be discussed in Chapter 7.) In the context of various forms of improvised work the distribution of different parts inevitably leads to the expectation of and need for a complex structure which may become difficult to manage for the teacher and pupils. Initiating a drama on the Fire of London by casting characters in roles as the king, the mayor, Pepys, etc. means that these characters have to assume differentiated roles and interact with one another convincingly. However, by asking pairs to enact the interview of the baker who is being questioned about his precise movements before going to bed on the fateful night (is he sure he put the fire out?), the initial demands are easier to manage. Alternatively, the class may take the role of investigators who are questioning a series of witnesses to establish the exact cause of the fire; this structure does not have to be based literally on pairs (a committee of investigators may be set up to pose the questions) but it follows the same dialogue/structural pattern of a confrontation between two antagonists.

Another consequence of distributing a range of parts is that there is an implied need for characterisation and individualised roles which is more demanding than the adoption of an attitude or the display of a particular viewpoint. If the pupils are asked to take on the role of the 'king's men who fought bravely to put out the fire' they have a concrete stance on which they can base their role and take cues from each other on how to sustain it. I am not arguing here that a concept of role (based more on the adoption of an attitude) should always take precedence over characterisation (based on a more rounded creation). There is a case to be made for the importance of character but it is important not to underestimate the practical difficulties of initiating and sustaining character.

Creating a narrative

The difference between narrative and plot was discussed in the previous chapter. Because narrative is the foundation of drama, it is natural to assume that the creation of a story is a necessary preliminary to engaging in drama. However, pupils can often produce creative and very imaginative ideas which they find difficult to turn into dramatic action. For example, instead of starting a drama based on 'Robin Hood' by inviting the participants to invent a story, Bolton placed the participants in pairs with a father teaching his son how to make arrows. Similarly, work based on 'Joseph and his Brethren' started with Joseph being interviewed years after the 'pit' incident (Bolton 1992a). This sort of approach arrests the rush towards episodic incidents.

Imitating the real world

It is an understandable consequence of exposure to a naturalistic form of drama on film and television to assume that the aim in drama is to replicate the real world as accurately as possible. Thus a teacher's instincts might be to want to perfect the miming of opening of doors, the drinking of tea, the counting of money. This is a complex issue because sometimes it is appropriate to focus on getting the action right but far less often than newcomers to the subject assume. Often the action of the drama needs to be subordinate to the meaning and content. Thus to begin a simple exchange between a husband and wife who are worried about their teenage child and subtlely inclined to blame each other for her wayward activities, it is not necessary to work out exactly how the mother will pour the tea into the teacup. It may be appropriate, however, to have the mother ironing while she speaks in order to symbolise the gender roles occupied in the household. It may be appropriate to focus on which person is sitting or standing if the dominance of one character is significant. When the action becomes important as signifier it is more likely to need to be the object of conscious attention. It might be appropriate also at times to direct the participants to engage in some action in order to help build belief in the situation or as a 'peg' for their acting. Knocking on an imaginary door, opening it and entering a room may be a helpful 'curtain raiser' for a formal interview between worker and boss but the accuracy of the miming is of no significance.

Directing the action

The assumption that the best way to initiate drama is for the teacher to take a major, intrusive role in directing the action ('speak more softly . . . try to walk more slowly . . . do not react so quickly') is educationally dubious because it is in danger of limiting the contribution of the pupils and their development of an understanding of both the content and dramatic form. It is also based on a very traditional and outmoded view of the theatre and director's role. According to Brook (1968: 17):

> In a living theatre, we would each day approach the rehearsal putting yesterday's dis-
> coveries to the test, ready to believe that the true play has once again escaped us. But the
> Deadly Theatre approaches the classics from the viewpoint that somewhere, someone
> has found out and defined how the play should be done.

The criticisms of theatre in the history of drama in education can largely be seen as a criticism of 'deadly theatre'. As with the other 'misconceptions' described here, it is not a question of outlawing any form of traditional directing completely but to recognise that as a starting point such an approach is more likely to make pupils self-conscious and over-dependent on the teacher.

Leaving pupils to their own devices

The over-intrusive direction of pupils in their drama is less likely to be found in schools these days because of the considerable influence of theories of self-expression in the 1950s and 1960s which made a virtue out of non-intervention by the teacher in the pupils' work. However, knowledge of pupils' capacity for dramatic play can lead to the contrary assumption that because drama is a natural activity pupils can be left to their own devices. As suggested earlier in this book, many approaches to drama recommended in the literature assume that pupils simply need to be told to make up a play or a scene.

Common problems

It is not uncommon to meet teachers who have attempted drama with a class only to abandon thoughts of ever trying to teach it again. Interestingly enough they often retain conviction about its value and popularity with pupils but have been put off by the difficulties they encounter. It will be helpful to give consideration to some of the problems teachers often encounter when starting drama work before discussing practical approaches and solutions.

Pupils fail to take the drama seriously

I think this is a more common problem with improvised drama than many books on the subject acknowledge. In some ways it should not be surprising because improvisation lends itself to the witty, unpredictable comment, the humorous aside, the parody. There has been a proliferation of programmes on radio and television based on improvisation techniques in which the goal is to entertain and amuse. Improvisation in the history of drama has often been associated with comedy. In North America there has been a growth of improvisation 'sports' as a form of witty entertainment and competition. Improvisation by its very nature demands the ability to think quickly and can therefore be threatening; it is not unusual for participants to find refuge in comedy and witticisms. Not of course that there is no place for comedy in the drama lesson, but it is the inappropriate response which teachers find wearing. This is another reason for variety in drama, interspersing improvised work with work on texts and script writing.

The drama fails to materialise

The cause can appear to be a lack of motivation but often derives from an inability to translate the idea into dramatic action. It is often a question of simply not knowing how to get started. It can also derive from an inhibition about sharing work if pressure to do so is exerted too soon. For every pupil who is eager to share their work and perform, there are others who are likely to find the whole process torturous and embarrassing. Awareness of the likely sensitivities of groups and individuals is one key to initiating successful drama.

Control breaks down

It is often more difficult for experienced teachers to start using drama because there is more at stake; for the beginning teacher who is already vulnerable, the exposure provided in drama is perhaps less of a threat. The question of discipline and control was discussed in the previous chapter where it was recommended that it is helpful to establish one's own thresholds as a teacher. It may help to clarify in one's own mind rules which need to be established prior to the drama. Many writers on drama have rightly emphasised the need to control and deepen the drama from within but that should not inhibit teachers from making clear what their expectations are over certain issues. For example, if pupils are to perform for each other it is vital that they respect each other's work and strict rules about making comments during performances may be necessary.

Working in pairs

The sorts of negative outcomes described above arise for a variety of reasons: the content is too remote from pupils' experience; the drama is based more on conflict than tension; the activity is introduced too suddenly; there is confusion over expectations. The advantage of pairs structure is that it offers a secure start for all participants because the work is relatively private. It also places a limit on the inclination to devise over-sophisticated narratives which is the tendency of large group work. Starting with pairs work allows the teacher to work to a preplanned structure. As suggested in Chapter 3 on planning, drama does not always lend itself to set routines and the best work often requires negotiation and flexibility. Pairs work (either improvised or scripted) provides a more secure structure for teachers as well as pupils in that a sequence of activities can be devised which culminate in handing over more responsibility to the pupils. Here then are some considerations to be borne in mind when setting up improvised pairs work:

- It is sensible to assume that participants who are about to start a workshop, whether they are junior school children or adults, are likely to feel a mixture of excitement and tension ('Am I going to be embarrassed or made to look foolish?'). Initial exercises should seek to make the participants feel comfortable.

- Often when a teacher asks pupils to get into pairs the first problems are encountered before any drama starts because of the isolate in the class with whom no one will work. There is no simple, immediate solution to this problem which is a very real one in many classes. Sometimes a firm instruction to form a pair or threesome works but it is generally not a good idea to insist if pupils are resisting because the problem can easily become a confrontation between teacher and class. Sometimes it is possible to have the particular individual work with the teacher. If the class are clearly ostracising one individual in the group there may be a long-term problem here which may need to involve other staff in the school and is unlikely to be solved on the spot.

- Whatever the central exercise is (e.g. interviewing a Prime Minister in history, questioning a character from a novel) use warm-up role play exercises before the main task to help engage commitment. This gives pupils a chance to 'feel' their way into the activity before the central, more important role play. It also allows the teacher to assess how the pupils are responding to the work, whether they are cooperating with each other or not. The problem with warm-up exercises is that they may not be very compelling for pupils. Here it is helpful to explain the purpose of the activity and the eventual direction of the work. An opening exercise might simply be to have one partner tell the other about the morning's journey to school. So instead of 'Tell your partner about a journey to school ...', the teacher's instruction might be: 'We are going to do three different very simple exercises to help get us warmed up and ready for drama.' Other useful introductory exercises (telling a fanciful version of the journey to school, giving an excuse for being late, returning a faulty item to a shop, interviewing an eye-witness to an accident) can be used literally to break the silence in comfortable, non-threatening ways without making too many demands on pupils and without launching prematurely into the central activity.

- Try to envisage what the pupils will actually do and say when they attempt the task. This is a good way of testing the appropriateness of what is being asked of them and is more difficult to do than it appears. In a history lesson the teacher had planned to ask pairs to 'act out the moment when the treaty was signed' but further reflection revealed that the task required little more than a miming action – there was no tension in the activity and no real possibility for verbal exchange. An activity of that kind might make the pupils feel self-conscious and find refuge in sending the occasion up. A more appropriate activity from the point of view of the drama would have been to have an adviser try to persuade the signatory of the treaty to change his mind moments before the signing (of course an activity which is appropriate to the historical context is needed).

- Using a preliminary instruction that pairs should 'decide who is A and who is B' in order to assign roles can save arguments. There is also a deeper reason for using this strategy in that it conveys the idea that choice of role is often arbitrary. The relationship between the real and fictitious context is complex but pupils need to be encouraged to adopt roles of different kinds.

- Everyone (pupils and adults) finds it easier to adopt roles in the early stages of drama which are close to their experience. That is why drama based on social realism involving families, discos, friendships, gangs tends to be so common with secondary pupils. It is important that the subject matter for drama is wide but initial pairs activities which are focused on familiar school and familiar domestic situations may be easier to enact and are thus useful starting points.

- It is not only the type of role (parent, slave, king) which determines the difficulty of the drama activity for the pupils but the situation in which they are placed. At first it may seem that thirteen-year-old pupils are likely to find it easier to assume roles of parents and teenage children who are having a disagreement over what time the pupil is allowed to come in at night than those of a king disagreeing with his chancellor about taxation. However, the two exchanges have similarities in that they both entail persuasion. Contrast these situations with one in which one parent is asked to comfort a child for some reason. In drama 'comfort' is more difficult to enact than 'persuasion' because in the former case one of the pair has too much of a passive role. 'Explaining' and 'telling' are legitimate warm-up exercises but do not work so well for actual drama. It is useful to begin a workshop for a group who are new to drama with exercises which are reflections of the group's own context: pupils (situations based on school); students (beginning a new course); teachers (parents' evening). In that case it is worth making clear what the purpose is ('let us start with an exercise which is close to everyone's experience').

- Sometimes it helps to supply intention and motivation to the characters. In the case of an interview: 'This job is important to you – if you don't get it you will have to cancel the holiday which your family has been expecting.' I once watched a lesson in which the teacher used an old coat to begin the drama, a good idea because it gave a concrete focus to the activity. The eventual aim was to create the character of the owner by making inferences about the appearance of the garment, contents of the pockets, etc. Two pupils volunteered to enact a scene in which the coat was found by them. Although the pupils were well motivated, the drama was disappointing because they found it difficult to do more than find the coat and pick it up. It would have been better to have given each of the pair a particular attitude ('one of you is very reluctant to touch the coat for fear of being accused of stealing it, the other is keen to pick it up and search the pockets').

- It is helpful when planning pairs activities to decide whether it is necessary to specify the outcome of the improvisation. In the example given above of finding a coat the pupils could be told that the coat will be picked up at the end of the scene – the tension derives in this case not from not knowing the outcome but by determining how that known outcome will be realised. Although spontaneous improvisations which are not preplanned can feel more real to the participants, it often helps to start with exercises which have a given outcome.

- As suggested earlier, it often helps to supply a 'peg' on which the participants can hang their acting. 'The newcomer to the flat is unpacking while the disagreement is taking place.' 'The boss keeps on working on his papers while he is questioning the employer about the theft.' The question of how and when it is appropriate to focus the pupil on particular actions relates to the overall meaning of the drama; giving pupils a clue as to what they might actually be doing while enacting a scene can help the quality of their work. 'While her mother is telling her to be careful on the journey, Little Red Riding Hood is arranging food in her basket.'

- It often helps to give a starting point which sets the appropriate mood for the exchange. It is surprising how many pupils who are new to drama simply do not know how to get themselves started. 'So your first line might be something like: "I know you don't want to talk about this but I think we have to . . ." (Head of House to pupil). "Could I take a little of your time to ask you some questions – it is very important" (policeman on a house-to-house enquiry).'

- It is generally recognised that straightforward conflict situations tend to lead pupils to shallow, confrontational scenes. The key ingredient is tension. Instead of asking them to role play a situation in which a parent has spent a teenager's savings (which is likely to induce a shouting match) the teacher builds in a moral case on the parent's side (he needed a deposit on a family holiday and planned to pay it back). This is usefully seen as a matter of building in constraints (Bolton 1992a).

- Simple role play situations can remain at the level of simulation (e.g. practising job interviews) but they can be overlaid with greater depth: one of the interviewing panel used to have a relationship with the interviewee.

- Pupils can be helped to share their work by using an 'open door' or 'eavesdropping' technique whereby just a thirty-second snatch of conversation is heard. This is a valuable method of getting pupils used to sharing their work without placing too much pressure on any individual and without prematurely dividing the class into confident performers and those who are shy and reticent. By asking every pair simply to share their work for literally seconds a feeling of group sharing can be established which can form a valuable basis for future performance.

- It sometimes helps to have the class watch the work of a particularly successful pair or for the teacher to demonstrate with a pupil in the class, provided those who are being asked to share their work are happy to do so. Traditional emphasis on individual creativity has tended to deny teachers this simple technique of giving pupils examples of the type of work required. It is rare, however, for pupils simply to copy exactly what they observe after this kind of modelling.

- When pupils are writing script (in pairs or in larger groups) it is often a good idea to restrict them to a specific number of lines to bring more focus to the work.

Games and exercises

In the early days of drama in education, games began to dominate in some classrooms simply because they were so much easier to manage than the whole-group spontaneous improvisations which, to some drama purists, were the only legitimate alternative. It is important that games do not dominate a lesson – teachers have to have resolve and resist the rather pleasing response which often ensues when pupils clamour to have their turn. However, with a more balanced approach to drama it is possible to have a clearer view of the valuable but limited place games should occupy. They can provide a warm-up activity which allows the teacher to assess the response and social cohesion of the group and may be helpful in allowing teacher and class to move away from normal routines in a secure fashion. They can also in some circumstances help with specific skill acquisition particularly in relation to performance work (Barker 1977). It is sometimes helpful to draw pupils' attention to the skills required in playing a particular game, the need for cooperation, taking turns, etc. which can elevate the status of the game and the tone of this part of the lesson, providing the right context for drama work. More importantly, they can provide a method of initiating drama whereby the tension generated by the game feeds into the work.

It is worth considering why games are often so much easier to manage than drama because that provides some useful pedagogical lessons. Games have definite predetermined structures, very definite objectives and elements of tension which do not have to be generated purely by the feeling of the participants themselves.

Thus waiting for some important news may in context be a situation which is full of dramatic tension but it is difficult to enact without fairly developed acting skills. However, trying to tease out important news from someone who is trying to withhold it is easier to act because it has more tension in its external structure. Games operate through the higher authority of the external rules and conventions without the need for an internal dimension required by drama. Many drama writers have developed the analogy between games and drama (Watkins 1981). Recognition of the similarities and differences between games and drama is thus a valuable means of understanding how they can enrich each other. This theme will be developed not in abstract but in the context of describing four games which are quite popular in the literature of drama but are presented here in terms of their structure. The further reading section at the end of this chapter lists a number of publications which describe games.

Keys of the Kingdom

This game is one of the most common to be found in books on drama because it creates such automatic tension. There are a number of variations but one which minimises the potential for physical contact allows more potential for the game to be developed directly into drama. One pupil (A) is seated blindfold on a chair. Pupils take it in turns to creep forward to lift the keys without being heard. If they are caught (by A raising a hand) inside the circle drawn around the chair they have been unsuccessful. If A raises a hand while they are outside the circle or if they manage to get the keys undetected the successful pupil takes over A's place as guardian of the keys. The game demands silence, intense listening and stealth. It can easily be translated into a make-believe situation by removing the guardian and asking the pupils simply to imagine the fictitious context, e.g. an escape from prison. This time the pupil creeps forward for the keys and, although there is no real possibility of being caught as there was in the game, has to behave as if there is. This is creating a limited dramatic situation based for the moment on external action rather than creating a context of genuine motivation but it is a useful way of initiating drama which can lead to a complete project. A lesson used to introduce the theme of dinosaurs with a Year 4 class which used this game as its starting point is described in Chapter 9. The structure here is based on the retrieval of something valuable which is important to the well-being or survival of the group.

Killer

The pupils sit in a circle. A 'detective' sits in the middle. The teacher chooses the killer by touching one of the pupils on the back while everyone else keeps their eyes closed. It is the killer's job to wink at people in order to kill them without being noticed by the detective. When killed, people fold their arms. The focus here for discussion can be the way in which the group becomes skilled at confusing the detective – seeking to get themselves killed, waiting for a while before announcing that they have been killed. Also it can be interesting to speculate on the different ways the detectives seek to determine the killer – it may be body language as much as actually trying to spot them in the act of winking. The game structure is based on discovery and deduction.

Charades

The aim here is to communicate information to the group without speaking and is based on the original party game in which the information was usually the name of a book, television programme or film and various signing conventions were established to indicate whether syllables, sentences or whole words were being mimed. However, the game can equally well be played by asking individuals to find ways of conveying increasingly complex messages without speaking and without necessarily using established conventions of any kind. In this way the game lends itself more easily to be developed into a dramatic situation whereby someone has important information to convey for some reason but without the capacity to speak. Here the constraint which contributes to both game and drama is that of withholding information.

Detective game

This game was described in the Introduction. The teacher or appointed member of the group acts as detective and questions the suspect to establish that the alibi is false. However, the part of the individual suspect is played by the whole class who have to listen to one another's responses so that a coherent story which does not contain contradictions is established. Played in this way there is far more interest and tension than if one individual is simply questioning another. It is the attempt to undermine the alibi formed by the group (although they are playing the part of one person) which gives the game its quality. It is the challenge to group cohesion which is a feature that can usefully be translated into drama when, for example, the town planner attempts to exploit the conflicting interests of the residents.

These are the broad structures underlying these games:

- retrieval
- discovery
- withholding information
- challenge to group cohesion.

These elements can be seen as helpful principles in structuring drama. If the group are devising a play about explorers the dramatic focus can be derived from their objectives – to get back stolen artefacts (retrieval), to find out what the uncharted territories contain (discovery), to keep their promise not to reveal the secret they uncovered (withholding information), to decide whether or not to trust their leader (challenge to group cohesion). An inexperienced class or group who are asked to create a play about explorers are likely to set about having a multitude of adventures without the necessary focus.

The term 'exercises' has already been used in this chapter to describe examples of work in pairs. It is often difficult to establish whether a particular activity properly counts as 'drama', 'game' or 'exercise'. As argued elsewhere in this book we should not expect to be able to establish completely discrete categories because language does not work in that way. Exercises tend to lack the structural tension that belongs to many games and are more useful as warm-ups and icebreakers. It is important to beware of making exaggerated claims for the power of particular activities: trust and concentration exercises do not guarantee trust or concentration. Exercises such as leading a partner around the room blindfold or over objects, walking around until a minute is thought to be up and then sitting down, shadowing the action of one's partner as if in a mirror, can create an atmosphere of quiet concentration but can also serve to move older participants from the security of chairs, ready for action. The decision whether games or preliminary exercises are thought to be necessary will depend much on the nature of the group and the choice of approach to drama, the subject of Chapter 5.

Further reading

Books by Winston, J. and Tandy, M. (2001) *Beginning Drama 4–11* and Neelands, J. (1998) *Beginning Drama 11–14* provide valuable reading for the beginner and experienced teacher. Bolton, G. and Heathcote, D. (1999) *So You Want to Use Role Play?* provides a guide to setting up role play. The following publications contain extensive descriptions of games and exercises, some of which are useful for drama but, as suggested above, they should only be used with a deliberate purpose in mind: Bond, T. (1986) *Games for Social and Life Skills*; Brandes, D. and Phillips, H. (1978) *Gamester's Handbook*; Brandes, D. (1982) *Gamester's Handbook Two*; Rawlins, G. and Rich, J. (1985) *Look, Listen and Trust*. A book which contains suggestions for games and activities but which is far more than that, an account of a radical approach to theatre, is Boal, A. (1992) *Games for Actors and Non-Actors*.

5

Approaches to drama

Categories

A CLASS OF YEAR 9 pupils is confronting the teacher in role as a politician at a press conference to find out more details about the cause of a recent train crash. Elsewhere in an infant classroom a similar scenario takes place but this time the pupils are confronting the teacher in role as a witch who is believed to have stolen a baby from the village. In the same school in the hall a group of pupils from Year 6 are rehearsing a mime sequence to accompany a poem for an assembly without the help of a teacher. Are these examples of drama or theatre or dramatic playing? How do we categorise different approaches to drama?

It can be quite a bewildering task to try to make sense of the various ways in which approaches to teaching drama have been described. Terms such as 'dramatic play', 'role play', 'conventions', 'theatre' are straightforward enough in normal usage but they are often employed by writers on drama in particular ways to make fine distinctions. If one adds to those terms the more idiosyncratic categories which have also been used to distinguish approaches to the subject, such as existential mode, mantle of the expert, then the picture becomes even more complex. To the critic or literary scholar versed in distinctions in drama between expressionism, naturalism, symbolism, the absence of reference to such variations in much of the literature on drama teaching may be a source of confusion. The purpose of this chapter is to offer a perspective on approaches to drama which will help teachers in choosing priorities in the classroom and which will assist in further reading on the subject. The aim is to seek clarity while avoiding over-simplification.

It was suggested in Chapter 1 that it is more helpful to recognise that categories are formed for a particular purpose than to argue in a vacuum that one type of categorisation is better than another. Approaches to drama can be distinguished using different criteria and for different reasons. Categories have been formulated in the past on the basis of the external form of the drama, the aims of the teacher or indeed the feelings of the participants. Particular criteria sometimes underlie approaches to categorising drama without these always being evident. It is also worth noting that certain categories can be formulated or taken as given while concealing other possibilities and priorities. If we distinguish between role play, dramatic playing and improvisation as forms of creative drama it begs the question of whether 'responding to drama' (i.e. the watching and analysis of plays) should also be a teaching priority.

As described in Chapter 1 the approach to drama in schools narrowed considerably in the 1950s and early 1960s largely through the influence of Slade, in whose work the predominant emphasis was placed on dramatic playing, sometimes referred to by other writers as improvisation. Thus in 1965 Courtney was able to proclaim improvisation as the kernel of drama in schools.

Whether it is called 'dramatic playing', 'improvisation' or 'role play' the approach to drama in schools, both as subject and method, which has been highly dominant involved pupils in the creation of drama without the use of scripts. However, a key to understanding how drama in education developed in the 1970s and 1980s is to recognise that there was an attempt to distinguish between types of improvised drama on the basis of the quality of the work, often using different terminology to do so. This is a key element in understanding the history of drama in education.

Whereas for Slade dramatic playing had been the supreme manifestation of child drama, the term 'play' later became one of disparagement for work which did not reach the required quality. Thus the teacher who relies on dramatic playing 'encourages by default, the development in his pupils of the habit of wallowing in meaningless playing . . .' (Bolton 1979: 29). Writers sought to define those qualities which elevated the experience of the participants in drama above mere playing. What underlay those attempts to distinguish drama from play was the recognition that drama can offer shallow or deep experiences, may or may not have aesthetic form, and needed the deliberate intervention of the teacher to take the work beyond the realms of play. While exponents of drama in education were claiming to have as their goal a quality of experience which could justifiably claim to be described as 'drama as art' its critics have claimed that by neglecting play text, performance and elements of theatre craft the art form has been ignored. A crucial distinction then in the history of drama's development is that between 'drama' and 'dramatic playing'. However, before examining those categories in more detail it will be necessary to consider the problems involved in defining the concept of drama itself.

Defining drama

It will not be the intention of this discussion to offer yet another definition of drama to add to those already formulated by other writers. The emphasis instead will be to draw attention to some of the confusion which can arise when the term is used in particular ways. The history of drama teaching is full of comments about the failure to define drama satisfactorily. The first DES survey in 1967 found it surprising 'to find how much time is being devoted in schools and colleges to a subject of whose real identity there is no real agreement' (DES 1967: 2). Typical of later writers was the comment that 'much misunderstanding and disagreement still exists as to the nature of drama in education' (Male 1973: 9). The problem with prescriptive definitions is that they often define boundaries in such a way that does not seem to represent adequately the way the term is actually used. The HMI document *Drama 5–16* offered a helpful account of what is to be counted as drama: 'It ranges from children's structured play, through classroom improvisations to performances of Shakespeare' (DES 1989: 1) The description which recognises that there is a continuum from a child's early play to theatrical productions on a grand scale is helpful because of its inclusive quality. However, it may not ring true to describe the spontaneous play of infants in the home corner as 'drama'. Similarly we might want to claim that the essential factor which distinguishes drama is that of 'pretending to be someone else' but feel reluctant to include the antics of a mimic as qualifying as drama. We should not be surprised that it is difficult to find a simple definition which embraces all uses of the term because language operates in a fluid way with overlapping boundaries.

What is perhaps more helpful is to understand the different ways in which the term 'drama' is used and to be thus armed against conceptual confusion which can easily arise when there is a slide from one use of the term to another. When 'drama' simply refers to the subject on the curriculum then it is likely to embrace all sorts of activities such as warm-up exercises, improvisations, watching plays, games and other related activities. Hirst (1974) made a useful distinction between a teaching 'activity' and 'enterprise', the latter term referring to a whole programme of work as opposed to one single activity. Thus 'drama' as an enterprise is likely to include a number of activities all of which are legitimately entitled to be called drama as long as they do not dominate. That distinction is quite important because it prevents the condemnation of a particular lesson or portion of a lesson simply on the grounds that 'it is not drama'. Warm-up exercises and games, play-reading and rehearsal which may constitute part of a lesson or part of a drama programme of study need to be judged in context.

It also should be recognised that the term 'drama' is sometimes used to make qualitative judgements. Thus when Bolton (1992a: 39) describes a drama lesson which he observed based on the story of Moses bringing the Israelites out of Egypt, the term 'playing' is used to describe work which does not qualify as drama. The class had been sent off to different parts of the hall to report back on whatever they found. 'After about five minutes they clustered round their teacher full of chatter, competing with each other in terms of what they had seen by way of rivers, hills, rich soil, wildlife, domestic animals, vegetation or the lack of them, etc. Not surprisingly the teacher, bombarded in this way, found herself pleading, "One at a time so I can hear".' Bolton goes on to observe, 'Pause to analyse what is going on and you discover a kind of "playing" that fails to be dramatic. Certainly the children are adopting an existential, "here and now" mode, but it should not be mistaken for drama for there is little that gives the participants (either consciously or unconsciously) a sense of form.' He goes on to describe the rest of the lesson where the children are given in contrast a more ritualistic and theatrical experience which does count as drama on his terms. The distinction between 'drama' and 'play' is an important one which needs to be considered in more detail.

Dramatic playing

As stated in Chapter 2, part of drama's motivating power is that it has its origins in the propensity of young children to engage in dramatic playing. The home corner is an important focus in many infant classrooms for the adoption of roles and the playing out of various situations. It should already be clear now that it will not be possible to provide a precise way of demarcating 'drama' from 'dramatic play' because language simply does not work in that way. It will, however, be possible to indicate broad characteristics of the two concepts. A particular example of a four-year-old 'playing' doctors with an adult is interesting for the degree to which it more closely resembles 'drama' than 'dramatic playing'.

The full transcript of the 'play' (for that is what it closely resembles) is given in Appendix A. The young child had previously been ill and had made a visit to the doctor's a short time before this exchange. Here the child adopts the part of the doctor and the adult that of the sick child. The doctor makes three visits to the house on three successive days with the health of the child deteriorating each time until finally he dies. What appeared to be at first a straightforward example of a young child imitating the manner and behaviour of a doctor – 'Open up your mouth. Open up your mouth. Let me see what's in it . . . Thank you . . . Right, we're not going to have an injection' – takes on more significance as concepts of death and burial are explored. The actual play lasted 20 minutes with no interruptions: the transcript is complete and unedited. Notice, it is the child who at times steps outside the drama to direct the action: 'Then you tell the little boy . . . Then you be the little boy . . . Tomorrow you're very, very poorly . . . Then you phone up . . .' Despite being completely absorbed in the activity there is a full awareness throughout that this is a fiction, being consciously crafted by the participants. There is a strong sense of narrative development as the health of the sick child deteriorates, which happens crucially at a very restrained pace. The sequence of events reaches a climax (as the boy dies) and resolution (as he is brought back to life). However, this 'resurrection' is very different from the way in which characters die and come alive instantly in the rough and tumble of infants' play: it is considered and ritualistic. The play ends as it began with the intention to play doctor thus giving the whole sequence an aesthetic unity. The self-referential moment adds to the feeling of a finale with the curtain coming down on the proceedings. The tone throughout, which can only be heard on the audio-recording and cannot be fully appreciated from the transcript, is extremely serious and committed. In the course of the play there is no concern to communicate with an audience but there is conscious attention to the way actions signify meaning – the young child in the play carefully writes the name of the deceased on the cross to signify death and burial.

This example helps identify some of the features which tend to be characteristic of drama as opposed to dramatic play (the claim cannot be put more strongly than that):

- The consequences of actions have significance for subsequent developments. (In dramatic play there is a lack of attention to the consequences of actions – people die and come alive, super heroes acquire incredible powers very easily.)

- The activity has a structure which works towards fulfilment. (In contrast in dramatic play there is a 'to-and-fro' movement which is not tied to any goal which would bring the activity to an end.)

- There is conscious awareness of the process of signification without necessarily an intention to communicate to an external audience, although this is often a tacit motivation. (In dramatic play there is absorption in the activity for its own sake with little such conscious awareness.)

- Dramatic focus and form serve to shape the activity to give it an aesthetic quality. (In dramatic play there tends to be a movement which renews itself through repetition: a child merely playing doctors might enjoy the constant return to injecting the patient.)

- In the drama there is a narrative but its progress is controlled. (In dramatic play the narrative is not measured and restrained but develops more according to the whim of the participants.)

- In the drama the language has a deitic form, using first and third person pronouns 'I' and 'you' frequently, with an elevated style using complete sentences. (In dramatic play the language has less of an informative function and is therefore more prone to the repetition and false starts which characterise normal speech.)

From the example it can be seen that dramatic play more closely resembles drama when it acquires theatre form (leaving aside for the moment the question of performance). And crucially when drama moves beyond dramatic play it needs to be *taught* as a dramatic art form. This was rarely acknowledged in the drama in education literature when the emphasis was placed more on the teacher's knowledge of dramatic form and ability to structure drama. As suggested in Chapter 3 on planning there is no *necessary* loss of emphasis on significant content and meaning. My own research (Fleming 1999) demonstrated that when a highly motivated group of pupils were left to their own devices devising drama in response to a stimulus they were unable to do more than resort to playing and engaged in activity which in a full class could easily have been interpreted as misbehaviour. The concept of 'quality' is crucial in relation to judging pupils' drama work (which I would suggest is less appropriate when referring to children's play). Where writers on drama have differed is in their description of how that quality is achieved and how it is best described, a matter for discussion in Chapter 9.

Choice of approach

Quality in drama then is an essential objective but is not, as implied in past and present controversies, the sole prerogative of only one way of working whether it be performance of play texts or spontaneous improvisation. Once it is recognised that a number of contextual factors are likely to influence the teacher's decision over which approach to drama to use, the attachment to a particular dogmatic position will be weakened. For example, young pupils are likely to achieve higher quality work when engaged in whole-group, strongly teacher-led, drama where the movement from dramatic playing to drama is more subtle.

In making appropriate choices for the type of work to be undertaken in the classroom or drama studio, broad decisions will need to be made with respect to orientation, organisation, mode and techniques. A system of categorisation of this kind is helpful in ensuring balance and variety when planning schemes of work.

– orientation: making, performing, responding

– organisation: pairs, small group, whole group

– mode: script, planned improvisation, unplanned improvisation

– techniques/conventions: tableau, questioning in role, etc.

In the account which follows, recommendations will be given about the appropriateness of particular approaches with respect to teaching aims (particularly when drama is being used across the curriculum) and the experience of the teacher (distinguishing between high and low risk approaches).

Orientation

The Arts Council of Great Britain (2003) identifies three attainment targets for drama: performing, making and responding. These provide a helpful way of thinking about broad approaches to the subject. The concept of 'orientation' rather than 'attainment targets' has been used here simply to indicate that these categories are valuable when drama is taught as both subject and method. In the latter case emphasis is likely to be placed more often on 'making' but not exclusively so. Chapter 8 contains an example of a curriculum project derived from work which had a strong performance orientation. The distinction between 'making' and 'performing' is more often one of emphasis, as indicated in Chapter 1; sharing of work in some form is likely to be a major component of almost all drama projects.

For a long time 'responding to drama' was ignored as an aim in drama teaching because the emphasis was more on creativity and self-expression. Of course, it could be argued that involvement in the creation of drama is a means of educating the ability to respond to drama; post-structuralist writing, including reader-response theories which have emphasised the active, constitutive role of the reader in the creation of meaning, lend credence to that view. The importance of having pupils reflect on the drama in which they have been involved has been a significant feature of drama practice, with writers frequently asserting that it is in the reflection that learning actually occurs. However, the tendency has been to place emphasis on the content of the work rather than the way the drama achieves meaning through signification. Table 5.1 shows the different emphasis on content and form.

TABLE 5.1 Examples of questions to elicit response to drama

Emphasis on content	Emphasis on form	Integrating content and form
Why did the character behave in that way?	What was the style of the acting?	What was the most important moment in the play and how was that moment marked?
What other methods could have been used to solve the problem?	How was the performance space used?	How were you made to feel sorry for that character?
Who was responsible for causing the argument?	What atmosphere was created by the lighting?	Why was that information important and how was it conveyed in the play? In what way was tension created and how did that affect our response to the incident?

It is the emphasis on the element of theatre craft devoid of reference to content to which writers on drama have taken exception (Neelands 1991). Responding to drama will be discussed in more detail in Chapter 9.

Organisation

It has already been suggested in the previous chapter that pairs work is a useful way of organising a class, particularly at the beginning of engagement in drama, because it provides security for the participants within a structure which places a natural curb on the excesses to which inexperienced pupils are sometimes prone in their drama. It should be noted that pairs work (which tends to be employed exclusively for exercises and role play activities) can equally be used in other modes such as scripted and devised improvisations. The other two basic methods of organisation are in small groups or as a whole class. An important point here is to note the absence of work on an individual basis as a category. There are occasions when individual exercises might be set as a preliminary task but it is not possible to teach drama on this basis because it is essentially a social, group activity.

1. Whole-group work

Whole-group work often with teacher in role gained prominence in the 1970s and 1980s partly as a reaction to the predominant method of directing pupils into groups to prepare and show a play. There is no doubt that improvised work of the highest quality can take place when the class are participating as a whole group with a common focus but the approach demands a considerable amount of concentration from the class and the pressure on the teacher can be high. I observed a lesson based on a shipwreck at sea in which the enthusiasm of the class broke into a flurry of disorganised activity with sailors and passengers jumping into the sea, swimming from sharks and generally enjoying themselves. The lesson was an illustration of the fact that verisimilitude is not necessarily the appropriate goal in drama. In reality the commotion on the boat would have been confusing and disorganised but for the drama to succeed it needed more control and focus. On the second occasion the teacher started the lesson by interviewing the survivors of the shipwreck (the whole class) months after the incident with a view to establishing the cause of the disaster. As part of the investigation they reconstructed where they were and what they were doing at the precise moment the disaster struck, in effect creating a play within a play. The structure (which represented a move away from dramatic play) allowed for more coherent drama work, more appreciation of the way drama functions and more focus on content. This approach combined the advantages of whole-group spontaneous improvisation (engagement, immediacy, uncertainty, excitement) with the pragmatic and educational benefits of more crafted work. Even whole-group work with a class, which appeared successful at the time, on reflection often reveals that only a small group of pupils sustained the drama. It is therefore more usefully used in combination with other structures and techniques, often to engage a group at the start of some work. Thus the drama based on UFOs described in Chapter 9 began with pupils in role as members of a government agency set up to investigate reported sightings. Much of the subsequent work took place in small groups but the teacher was able to establish the context and build belief in the early stages.

2. Small-group work

There have been several references so far to the mistaken assumption that all groups need to be told is to 'create a play'. That does not mean, however, that group work is not a valuable means of organising classes for drama. On the contrary, it is likely to be one of the most common structures for pupils of junior school age and beyond because it places emphasis on devising and offers clear opportunities for responding. It is important to recognise, however, that the way group work is initiated is a key to its success and that one of the aims should be for pupils to acquire the ability to structure their drama in groups. The following list provides suggestions for ways in which teachers can seek to elevate the quality of small-group work.

- Vary the groupings so that the same friendship groups are not always working together. This can provide a fresh impetus to the work as long as it does not alienate the class. Agreement to do so could be procured in advance and then simple lots drawn to create new groups. Often pupils appreciate the teacher's intervention to ensure mixed-sex groups if they as a class are inhibited from working in that way.

- Restrict the focus of place and time (the old Aristotelean unities). Sometimes pupils' drama becomes confused because they try to locate the action in too many places and cannot cope with the changes. A drama about the gunpowder plot which has to take place entirely in the home of one of the plotters presents a different type of challenge.

- Impose other constraints, e.g. restrict the use of physical space, give a time limit for preparation, ask for the scene to be enacted without words, without physical contact.

- Make it clear in advance whether the intention is that the work will be performed to the rest of the class. Group work does not always have to be shared in this way (although this provides a valuable motivating factor) but the aim should be clear from the start.

- Ask the pupils to plan the outline of the drama and share the scenario in advance of enacting it so that it can be subject to critical discussion by the teacher and rest of the class, who can seek to anticipate possible difficulties. They can also be encouraged to share 'rough drafts' which can be subject to critical advice.

- Pupils can be encouraged to use non-naturalistic conventions in their own small-group work (see Chapter 6). Techniques such as questioning in role, articulating characters' thoughts and using a character to relate part of the narrative can be used to deepen the work.

- Instead of setting small-group drama work as a topic – e.g. 'in small groups prepare and perform a play about theft' – set it as a more focused task: 'show the circumstances which caused an unlikely person to indulge in theft'. As with pairs work described in Chapter 4, tension can be injected from the start to help the pupils construct the drama. Instead of 'the prisoners decide to escape', 'the prisoners decide to escape but one of the inmates is reluctant to go along with the idea'.

- Encourage pupils to work out exactly how the drama will begin and end and explore different ways of doing so explicitly. When pupils perform their planned improvisations they often are unable to bring them to a conclusion.

- If appropriate, ask the groups to end the scene by posing a question to the rest of the class, e.g. 'Was the king right to take that decision?'

- Ask groups to show two different endings with alternative ways of resolving the drama.

- Lighting, music and props will enhance almost any piece of drama but they have to be used sparingly to be effective. Pupils tend to overuse them if given a free rein because they become a substitute for working on the meaning of the work.

- Ask the groups to work first of all on some element which will be used (when perfected) in the group drama, e.g. a news broadcast, a press conference, a moment of physical action such as a fight sequence.

Table 5.2 provides examples of ways in which group work can be given focus and provides specific drama objectives (adapted from Fleming 1997).

TABLE 5.2 Providing focus in group work

Focus	Drama objective
Alternative perspective	Providing two perspectives on an event, e.g. a dream is contrasted with how things actually happened; two versions are provided of how a window was broken.
Analogy	Work on a parallel scene which represents the main theme: pupils are left alone in a classroom to 'get on with their work' to parallel the plot of *Lord of the Flies*.
Beginnings	Focus on ways of starting drama: direct address to audience, uses of voices off-stage, use of actions, delaying entrance of main character.
Counterpoint	Placing two scenes or extracts side by side to enhance meaning: the reading of a negative school report is set against a scene from the pupil's home life.
Endings	Focus on ways of ending drama: use of ambiguous endings, tableaux, song, lights, ritual, stage action.
Exposition	Working out how to convey the necessary context (characters, place and time) without resorting to narrative or prologue and how to withhold information to create interest.
Externalising inner conflict	When a character is facing a conflict (e.g. Proctor in the last Act of *The Crucible*) different courses of action are voiced out loud.
Framing action	Actions provide extra information for the audience before the dialogue begins, e.g. the mayor in 'The Pied Piper' pours himself a drink, lights a cigar and hides both when he hears a knock at the door.
Incongruity	Unusual characters and situation are combined for comic and satirical effect: a fairy-tale character in a counselling session being interviewed by police.
Irony	The dialogue conveys more meaning to the audience than the characters realise.
Minor characters	A perspective is given from minor characters: a play about Goldilocks and the three bears begins with her neighbours being interviewed about her.
Off-stage action	An oblique approach in which the main action happens 'off-stage' – e.g. a restaurant or dinner party is seen from the point of view of the events in the kitchen.
Time shift	Events are presented in a non-linear way: the events of the Prodigal Son begin with the son returning home after his travels; the story of the Pied Piper begins with the unveiling of a memorial to the children.

Mode

In describing different modes of drama I am using 'improvisation' as a generic term to include all examples of drama in which pupils work without a script. Approaches to work with script and the reasons for its neglect will be dealt with in Chapter 7. The important distinction here, then, which needs some consideration is that between 'planned' and 'spontaneous' improvisation. As with almost every other conceptual distinction discussed so far the difference is one of emphasis.

In some ways the idea of a 'spontaneous improvisation' is a tautology because spontaneity is at the heart of what it means to improvise. However, the degree to which the context is determined in advance of the drama can vary considerably. In extreme cases there is no prior planning at all. 'Walk-in' drama works by having the class sit in a circle with one pupil in the middle. A second pupil enters the circle and begins an improvisation, followed by a third and fourth, with each one contributing to the situation which was originally defined. There is no discussion of how the work should unfold and the challenge of the 'game' or 'exercise' is to get as many pupils into the circle as possible. The technique can be a useful one for collecting several ideas which might be used as the basis for a drama project. A similar exercise can take place in pairs with one person having to respond imme-diately to the advances of the other.

At the other extreme is a form of improvisation in which the context, the char-acters and the outcome are all predefined. Thus a pairs improvisation might be set up in such a way which assigns roles to the characters (father and teenage daugh-ter), defines the time and place (it is eleven o'clock at night in the kitchen of their house), the context (the daughter arrives home one hour later than expected), the situation (they have a row but try not to wake the rest of the family asleep in the house) and the outcome (the daughter storms off to bed saying she is going to run away). It remains for the participants to improvise the dialogue which results in the designated outcome. A less extreme form of preplanning would be to define every aspect of context except the outcome and this approach to drama has been central in thinking in drama in education, particularly in its early stages when 'surprise' was considered to be a key element.

As with whole-group work, spontaneous improvisation (in the sense of not defining the outcome), because it has the quality of experiencing the drama at life's pace, has the potential for some of the most deeply felt and enriching work. However, it is not without its risks and its limitations. Sometimes reality (which is always present) can impinge too much on the fictitious context of the drama. This can be observed when pupils seize on some aspect of the environment (e.g. a pic-ture on a wall) in order to support the drama, often in a way which damages the integrity of the work. More seriously, the drama may be used to disguise teasing or may leave the participants with an awkward feeling of ambiguity. 'You're really thick' says one person to another in role and the recipient is left wondering to what degree he was being addressed as himself. Sometimes spontaneous improvisation can feel like an awkward social occasion when everyone is gamely trying to keep the conversation going. Another consideration with work of this kind is that because the emphasis is more on experiencing the drama there is less focal awareness on its creation, on the process of signification; when the outcome of the drama is known in advance pupils are more at liberty to focus not simply on the meaning but on the way meaning is created.

It is also possible to question that tradition of placing 'planned and unplanned improvisation' in one totally separate category and 'script' in another (a theme to which we will return at the start of Chapter 7).

Techniques/conventions

For teachers who use drama across the curriculum, making drama is likely to be the primary (but not the only) choice of orientation. As stated in the previous chapter pairs work provides a fairly secure structure, and planned improvisation presents fewer risks than spontaneous work. However, in choosing an approach a decision will have to be made about choice of technique or convention, which will be the subject of the next chapter.

Further reading

For accounts of varied approaches to drama see edited collections by Hornbrook, D. (ed.) (1998b) *On the Subject of Drama* and Nicholson, H. (2000) *Teaching Drama 11–18*. Hahlo, R. and Reynolds, P. (2000) *Dramatic Events* provides guidance on running drama workshops. See Frost, A. and Yarrow, R. (1990) *Improvisation in Drama* and Johnstone, K. (1981) *Impro* for books on improvisation. For an account of Heathcote's distinctive approach to drama in the 1970s see Wagner, B. J. (1976) *Dorothy Heathcote: Drama as a Learning Medium*. A useful summary of various drama debates in the mid-1980s including criticism of different approaches can be found in an article by Byron (1986).

6

Drama techniques and conventions

Basic approaches

IN A YEAR 5 classroom the class are busy working on the theme of bullying. They have created two still images in which the bully in the first is the victim in the second. In a nearby secondary school a Year 9 class are creating still images showing the position of the characters when a particular line is spoken from a Shakespeare play they are studying. Elsewhere a Year 11 class have begun their work on the theme of old age by creating still images showing the moment when the grandparent has to leave the extended family to go into a home. There is little doubt that the convention of using still images is used extensively (perhaps over-used) in drama lessons and it will be clear from the examples that it is not easy to see a clear progression in the use of drama form. The advantages and limitations of seeing drama teaching in terms of discrete conventions is one of the themes which will be explored in this chapter.

The more open-ended approach to drama advocated by Slade in the 1950s was given a more tightly controlled and systematic methodology through the use of various exercises and structures advocated by Way. The latter's 1967 book *Development Through Drama* was extremely popular and sold widely precisely because it offered teachers ready-made formulae for lessons over which the teacher had considerable control. There is a recent parallel in that the approach to drama advocated by Heathcote and Bolton has been made more accessible to teachers by the employment of drama 'conventions' or 'techniques'. The advantage of packaging drama into a series of discrete activities which can be employed selectively by the teacher is clear; the process of facilitating successful drama work is made less mysterious and rather more easy to realise. There are, however, similar dangers in that dramatic activity may be reduced to a form of mechanistic and easily replicated, discrete techniques with insufficient attention to particular contexts and situations and less emphasis on unity and the process of play-making.

The term 'conventions' in drama teaching is sometimes used very widely to refer to the way the class is organised (small group or whole group), various ancillary activities (writing, research) or to dramatic and pedagogic techniques selectively used in the course of the lesson as a part of a drama project or as a separate activity (teacher in role, questioning in role, forum theatre). It is the latter use of the term which will be the main focus of this chapter but it will be helpful to explore briefly other related uses because these point the way to a more coherent use of conventions.

The term 'convention' in the context of the theatre is used to refer to those aspects of the art form which are not real but are accepted as such as part of the fictitious context. Drama and theatre can only operate by virtue of particular conventions which derive from the willing suspension of disbelief. Participants need to accept that when one actor 'kills' another on stage the victim does not actually die. The use of soliloquy observes the convention that other characters on stage who are closer to the speaker cannot hear the speech. It was a convention in the Elizabethan theatre to accept males as playing the part of females. The advent of realism in the nineteenth century can be seen in part as an attempt to diminish or conceal conventions considered to be unlifelike. Brechtian and other forms of modern drama violated traditional conventions of theatre by laying bare the process by which the illusion was created, thus in turn creating new conventions. The importance of considering the concept of convention in this sense, in isolation from the wider term often used in drama in education, is that it is helpful to understand that the types of convention pupils will more readily accept are ones derived from the drama to which they are exposed within their culture, largely drawn from television. Thus flash-back as a convention of distorting time-scale is readily accepted by pupils, although the means of communicating the idea is usually drawn from film techniques and is difficult to realise in drama. It is for the same reason that pupils bring the 'fourth wall' convention (the attempt to represent life in a naturalistic way with photographic exactitude) to their understanding of drama. Using 'convention' in this narrower sense helps retain a historical perspective on drama and recognises that certain conventions have dominated at different times. More importantly in the context of drama teaching it acknowledges that for cultural reasons certain conventions tend to be accepted more readily than others.

It is easy to take for granted that drama relies on accepting the major convention of operating in an 'as if' or 'pretend' mode. It is second nature for young children to adopt roles in their dramatic play, to switch roles easily and to accept the roles of others. In the doctor's visit drama described in Chapter 5 the four-year-old readily accepts the change of role from doctor to mother and briefly comes out of role to direct the play in the space of minutes without inhibiting the flow of the action.

CHILD (as doctor): Here you are. Let's go in your house. Say hello to your mummy.

ADULT (as sick child): Hello mummy. I'm better.

CHILD (directing outside drama): Make your mummy talk.

ADULT (outside drama): Do you want to be the mummy?

CHILD (as mother): Hello.

ADULT : I'm better.

CHILD : How nice to see you. I just bought a little present for you while I was out.

The fact that the broad drama convention of adopting the make-believe mode comes so naturally to pupils explains why improvised drama is such a popular form in schools and why it was promoted in the early days of drama in education. It also shows why the necessity for teaching drama *per se* was underestimated because it seemed to come naturally to pupils. There is no guarantee, however, that pupils will accept all drama conventions as easily. It has been part of the tradition of drama in education to concentrate on the teacher's use of conventions to facilitate drama. Rather more emphasis, however, needs to be placed on the pupils' conscious understanding of dramatic techniques.

Some very comprehensive guides to the use of conventions have been published and details are given in the further reading section at the end of this chapter; it is not the intention to repeat unduly what has been written elsewhere. The purpose of this chapter is to describe some of the conventions which are likely to be most useful to the newcomer to drama and to give an account of how they might be best introduced to classes along with possible pitfalls to be anticipated. A theme of this chapter is also to focus on the degree to which pupils need to be helped to use conventions meaningfully. Examples will be given of how the different conventions can be used in different subjects and to further particular objectives. Various conventions, such as tableau and questioning in role, can be a useful means of helping pupils to read and respond to dramatic text, which will be dealt with in Chapter 6.

Tableau

'Tableau', 'photograph', 'sculpture', 'freeze frame', 'wax works', 'statues' are all terms used when the participants are asked to create a still image with their bodies either as individuals or more usually as a small group – whether to capture a moment in time, to depict an idea or to isolate a moment of the drama. Thus a group of Year 5 pupils who had created a play about rescuing a princess from a dragon had spent much of the drama negotiating with the dragon's unwilling keeper, the teacher in role. When it finally came to the fight with the dragon this was represented by three different freeze frames or mimed sculptures which they adopted to show the fight, thus avoiding the mayhem which might have ensued if they had tried to act out the confrontation and the potential disappointment if it had been avoided completely. The different terms used to describe this technique are helpful ways of introducing the activity to pupils and also give some indication of the ways in which the convention can actually be used within the drama. For example, pupils can be asked to depict the photographs which were taken of an event or incident ranging from a wedding to a murder or the sculpture which was built to represent the play *Dr Faustus*. These terms are usually used interchangeably but it makes a subtle difference of difficulty if the pupils are creating a two-dimensional photograph or a three-dimensional sculpture; the idea of creating a photograph is sometimes a relatively straightforward way of introducing the activity to a class.

It is clear from current literature on drama that this convention is widely used; in fact as suggested in the introduction to this chapter it is perhaps in danger of being overused, just as games at one time dominated some drama lessons, if as a result pupils do not have sufficient opportunity to engage in dialogue and play-making. There are some obvious pragmatic reasons why tableau should be so popular. The task culminates in silent, concentrated and focused work and is thus an attractive option from the point of view of control. It demands, and often promotes, group cohesion, and allows everyone to participate in some way whatever their level of skill or confidence. For the teacher who is new to drama it is a valuable activity because, although a technique which can be usefully employed within a drama, it can also be used on its own as a one-off exercise. There are also compelling aesthetic and educational advantages.

1 It freezes a moment in time and this can be an important corrective to the tendency pupils have to think exclusively in terms of narrative development.

2 Pupils are encouraged to focus on the way meaning is conveyed by subtle changes in expression, gesture, position. (Notice that to create this sort of focus in a spontaneous improvised drama sometimes runs the risk of ruining the flow of the work.)

3 When pupils are asked to create a tableau they are being asked to think about presentational skills in an unthreatening context.

4 It helps pupils learn how to condense meaning into a single moment and to read the full significance from a single moment. Successful drama works through condensation and compression through a process of aesthetic 'packing' which pupils can experience in a limited way in tableau.

5 Asking pupils to present a 'photograph' or 'freeze frame' can provide a useful means of representing situations in drama which might otherwise be beyond the scope of the lesson (e.g. the fight with the dragon, the football riot).

6 It can be a useful method of protecting participants by distancing them from moments which are potentially too difficult emotionally (e.g. instead of enacting the funeral, groups can depict the moment).

7 Because it culminates in stillness and silence it can, paradoxically, reveal the dynamism in a particular situation – drama which operates at 'real-life' pace often does not allow the participants or audience to dwell within a moment.

Although it is quite an accessible technique to use, there are considerations which it is useful to bear in mind:

- Pupils who are new to this way of working need to be inducted slowly, perhaps through mirror exercises, waxworks, photographs and so on. It helps to present a challenge: 'see how long you can hold the position without moving'. Whereas tableau used to its full effect contains tension and elements of its own future development, the initial exercises can simply be to show items like 'sports', 'jobs', 'hobbies'. Young pupils will enjoy playing the game of 'freezing'; older pupils may be a little awkward about holding the tableau with all the concentration it requires but when they are confident in doing so the results can be very satisfying.

- Pupils must learn the skill of holding and reading a tableau. It takes time – more than might be expected. Again it is useful to challenge the class to hold the image for a specific length of time as a way of motivating them. As with pairs exercises (Chapter 4) it is helpful to include preliminary exercises before the central focus.

- Include significant meaning and tension – e.g. instead of 'Create a photograph of a wedding' the instruction might be 'The photograph betrays that one member of the family felt very differently from everyone else.' Other qualifications which introduce elements of tension include: 'The physical positions indicate the status of the characters', 'The most important detail is the last we might tend to notice', 'Closer inspection of the image which we might not notice on first viewing reveals that . . .'

- Juxtaposition of a reading with the frozen image (whether poem, extract from a novel, someone's will, a letter) can have quite a powerful aesthetic effect and can deepen the work even though the tableau itself is very straightforward – e.g. the family gathered around the table to hear the will being read.

- When using more complex work such as conveying an abstract quality it is useful to have an example to show the class, perhaps through photographs.

- It is often helpful to make it clear whether the group must negotiate the tableau or (more rarely) one person is to direct the rest of the group to form the image. The latter instruction can be useful because it is sometimes difficult for a group to imagine what their work looks like.

- Taking an actual photograph of the work can be a useful record and provide motivation.

It is also important to know what to do with tableaux once they have been created. It is sometimes assumed that the only appropriate response is to attempt to guess what has been depicted. Unless pupils have been given another focus they will often start to do so when they view each other's work, sometimes with disappointing results to all participants if they are unable to explain fully everything they can see. Sometimes it is enough for pupils to display their work, possibly juxtaposed with a reading or narrative. The work can be developed by asking pupils to articulate characters' thoughts or voices. Alternatively a new image can be created related to the first – e.g. having created an image to represent their view of school, present another which shows school as they would like it to be. Tableaux can also be combined with elements of costume, lighting and stage design, thus introducing those elements of theatre craft in a secure context without the pressure of having to act. When pupils are experienced at using tableaux it can be used at all ages, but progression will derive from the wider context (including the content), the degree of independence given to the pupils and the other conventions used.

Questioning in role

Otherwise known as 'hotseating', questioning in role is perhaps one of the most useful techniques available to the teacher who is new to drama because it operates in such a controlled way. In its simplest form it involves one pupil or the teacher being questioned in role about his or her motives, character, attitude to other people and so on. As with tableaux, this is a convention which is 'non-naturalistic' and thus, as well as being a valuable pedagogical method, its use can be seen as part of the dramatic education of a class. In the context of play-making, it can be used to deepen characterisation or as a means of having pupils respond to a play they have watched by questioning the actors in role. As a teaching technique employed within other subjects it can be used on a one-off basis and thus is quite a secure introduction to the adoption of role for both teacher and class.

The Introduction described how this technique can be easily introduced by playing a simple detective game in which the pupils as a whole take the role of a suspect who is being questioned in order to try to break the alibi. The class can then assume the role of a character from fiction who is likewise questioned about motives and attitudes. Having experienced the question and answer technique within the security of being one of a large group, pupils may then be invited to adopt individual roles in order to be questioned by the rest of the class. As with tableaux, there are considerations which contribute to the success of this activity:

- Pupils sometimes remain at the level of asking literal, barely relevant questions but can be given a lead by the teacher's intervention – e.g. to the Prodigal Son: 'You have told us in some detail about what you did on your travels. Was your father equally interested in where you had been?'

- In a drama studio the questioning in role can be given considerable theatrical impact by placing the character in a spotlight and having the questions emerge from the dark.

- Sometimes the role of those asking the questions needs to be described (e.g. the peasants have the chance to ask the king about his new tax laws) but often they occupy a 'twilight' role which does not have to be defined; this is part of the acceptance of the convention. However, ambiguity can sometimes cause problems when a pupil who is being questioned becomes hostile and asks 'Why are you asking me all these questions?'

- If no questions are forthcoming or if they stop prematurely the class can simply be asked to discuss possible questions briefly in pairs before resuming.

- Problems can arise when a pupil does not have sufficient knowledge to sustain the role (e.g. a figure from history or a character from a novel). The same objectives may be achieved by having the pupil take the role of a minor character or bystander to an event who is not expected to know as much – e.g. instead of questioning Moses, the focus of attention may be one of the Israelites who went on the journey with him.

- Initial parameters of the role can be defined but it is important not to expect pupils to have to remember too much. A PSHE lesson on marriage was introduced by the teacher reading a letter from a wife to a marriage guidance counsellor. Pupils then volunteered to play the part of the wife and the husband, who were questioned by the rest of the class. The initial letter defined the context and character in a way which facilitated the questioning.

- Pupils who are being questioned can begin to display the feelings of the character (nervous, tense, wary, hostile) but it is important that the acting does not detract from the belief in the role.

- The questioning in role convention can be developed within a drama to symbolise repression (e.g. when a character is bombarded with rhetorical questions).

- An empty chair can be used to represent the character so that both questions and answers can be supplied by the group.

Eavesdropping

This technique is also sometimes called 'spotlighting' or 'open door' and refers to a process whereby the whole class is asked to freeze, and small groups are asked to come alive and enact a moment from their drama while others observe. It was introduced in the section on pairs work (Chapter 4) and is a valuable method of having pupils become used to sharing their work without the pressure of acting out a complete scenario. Describing it as a 'basic approach' can be somewhat mis-leading because the strategy can be used effectively with more advanced drama structures such as spontaneous whole-group improvisation as described below. However, it is a basic way of introducing the sharing of work without inviting pupils to embark on performing rambling, embarrassing small-group plays.

- Pupils are asked to freeze during their small-group or pairs work and they come alive at the teacher's cue to continue the drama for a short time, perhaps for only 30 seconds. It is a good idea to give the pupils advance warning that this is going to happen.

- Alternatively, pupils may be invited to prepare the moment which will be 'spotlighted' in this way. This is a rather different technique and demands different skills – the pupils need to be able to prepare a short piece which conveys the essence of the scene but which appears to be part of a longer exchange. The pupils are being asked to replicate some of the skills of a playwright who will often convey the impression as the curtain rises that events are in full flow.

- In spontaneous whole-group drama when the class have dissipated to different parts of the studio the teacher can freeze the action and ask pupils to show what is going on in their scene. Thus in a play based on a village the teacher moves from shop to shop and house to house so that all pupils learn what is going on in different parts of the play.

Play within a play

At its most sophisticated, this is another strategy which could hardly be described as 'basic' but it can be employed in ways which help pupils to enact scenes in drama which would otherwise be too difficult for them. It is not literally using a play within a play in the way Shakespeare does in *Hamlet* or *Midsummer Night's Dream* but rather it borrows that convention to frame one fictitious context within another. Thus pupils may find it difficult to enact a Hindu wedding with the appropriate degree of commitment and seriousness but may find it easier to present a television documentary in which actors reconstruct moments from the wedding to go with the commentary. Asking pupils to prepare a documentary presentation on an event in history (the Fire of London) or an issue (animal rights) can be enhanced by having events reconstructed within the programme. Thus the last acts of the baker before going to bed and the act of breaking into the science laboratories can be rehearsed and presented as part of the documentary. The technique can be used as a distancing device. Participants may find it difficult to improvise a scene in which one person is trying to talk another down from a suicide attempt but they might find it more comfortable to take the part of police officers in a training session learning to do so. In a previous chapter a lesson was described in which a chaotic drama on a shipwreck was salvaged by having the pupils reconstruct the events in a television studio.

Advanced techniques

Teacher in role

It is likely that some readers will disagree with the distinction between 'basic' and 'advanced' techniques used here. That is as it should be because, as argued earlier, teachers have different thresholds, styles and aptitudes. Adopting a role within a drama can be for many teachers a most comfortable and natural activity but in my experience many newcomers to drama find it rather more threatening than much of the literature on the subject often acknowledges.

It is quite possible to teach drama effectively without this technique and indeed it is better to do so if there are major reservations about its use; pupils are quick to detect uncertainty and will not believe in the role if the teacher lacks confidence. As with other techniques it is one which can be overused with the result that pupils are given insufficient initiative for planning, advancing and shaping the drama (even with the adoption of a minor part, the teacher in role is very influential). It is likely to figure more prominently in drama with younger pupils. On the other hand, used appropriately, it is one of the most powerful techniques available to the teacher. In the past the degree to which teacher in role can be seen as a form of teaching drama using modelling has been underestimated.

1   It can make the drama more real for the pupils.

2   It can allow the teacher to demonstrate what is required in particular situations.

3   The drama can be deepened and the pupils can be challenged from within the drama – thus the teacher can pursue educational objectives without stopping the flow of the work.

4   The language of the drama can be influenced by the teacher's example.

5   The normal teacher – pupil relationship is renegotiated within the drama.

There is quite a large volume of literature available on the use of teacher in role (see further reading at the end of this chapter). In the section which follows therefore only a summary of some major pointers to the use of this strategy is given.

■   An intermediary role can be more useful than an authority role – not 'I am the boss' but 'I will have to ask the boss about that'.

■   Teacher in role can help individuals who are struggling with the drama – 'I believe, sir, that you wanted to mention the problem about the smoke'.

■   It is a good idea to signal the change back to teacher in some way to avoid confusion (e.g. a particular chair).

- Commitment from the pupils often does not come immediately but patience can pay dividends. When pupils appear not to be reacting positively to teacher's role, finding it unconvincing or even funny, it is often a question of teacher staying committed in a serious way and pupils gradually becoming involved.

- Pupils who are not involved can be drawn in by teacher in role – 'I wonder what those people are thinking'.

- The teacher can contribute to group work in role in order to deepen the work (e.g. as the group set up their premises in the village the teacher calls on them as a health inspector).

Using two teachers with one in role opens up all sorts of possibilities. In this case one teacher stays in role permanently and the other manages the class.

Mantle of the expert

As with teacher in role this technique was invented by Heathcote and her use of it is quite complex. It is described by Heathcote and Bolton (1994: 5) as a means by which 'theatre can create an impetus for productive learning across the whole curriculum'. In its most elaborate form it involves having the pupils take the role of 'experts' who are engaged in an enterprise, for example running a factory or an advisory service for some distant clients who never actually appear in the drama but communicate by letter or messenger. The curriculum learning takes place through the expert role when the pupils are called on to solve some problem or offer some advice to the clients. However, the key to this technique as used by Heathcote is that the expertise of the participants is established in detail and at great length before the engagement in the central focus of the work.

Thus a group who will eventually advise on bullying may first establish their expertise as education experts by advising on the best height for school chairs, the appropriate range of colours for school crayons or how to change a classroom to accommodate a blind pupil.

A less elaborate version of mantle of the expert is sometimes employed when pupils conduct an investigation or an enquiry in their role as archaeologists, historians or investigators. Thus in role as experts pupils were invited to investigate new documentary evidence which seemed to cast a negative light on the greatly revered, deceased King David. The evidence in question was the biblical story of David and Bathsheba torn into fragments, which the pupils had to sequence and then attempt to decode. The ethical issue here centred on whether the King's good name should be publicly destroyed, given his obvious repentance before his death.

Other techniques include forum theatre (in which the class as audience are involved in shaping the drama as it unfolds before them), sound tracking (in

which pupils invent sounds to accompany moments in the drama), and thought
tracking (pupils articulating aloud the thoughts of a character), and are dealt with
in more detail in some of the publications listed at the end of this chapter.

Retrieving strategies

It is difficult to anticipate how a class will react in a given situation and it is therefore difficult to reduce any form of teaching – let alone drama teaching, which
tends to be more open-ended and inclined to risk taking – to a series of set routines and exercises. The purpose of this section therefore is to indicate the types of
measures which can be taken when things start to go wrong and do not proceed as
planned. The emphasis here is not simply on retrieving a lesson but on ensuring
that standards of drama are sustained within a programme of work or when
drama is used on a long-term basis across the curriculum.

1 It is not unusual for teachers to engage in a rather unproductive post mortem
   after an unsuccessful drama which often results in pupils responding to
   teachers questioning 'what went wrong?' with the answer 'we just fooled
   about'. Such exchanges only serve to lower morale and should be avoided. An
   experienced class often can identify specific reasons why a drama did not work
   but very often the class are made to feel responsible for not being able to fulfil
   the particular task which was over-ambitious. It is a good idea to avoid
   recrimination but try to retain a positive attitude to drama.

2 Sometimes either in discussion or questioning in role pupils simply dry up. In
   such cases it can be useful to give them a moment in pairs to plan what they
   want to ask or say.

3 When asked to prepare work in groups to be shown at the end of the lesson, even
   the most carefully formulated task can result in some groups not being able to
   present anything. The teacher has to make a carefully balanced judgement to avoid
   reacting negatively to what may have been a genuine effort but also to avoid being
   indulgent. It may be enough to ask the groups to report on their idea.

4 There is no simple solution to the problem of groups working at different
   paces and some finishing well before others. As with any classroom task it is
   useful to have extension work in mind (e.g. an additional tableau, a
   questioning in role sequence, a piece of script) as discipline problems can arise
   if pupils are unoccupied.

5 Pupils often fail to take the drama seriously when belief has not been built in an
   appropriate way. However, there is no guarantee, no matter how careful the
   teaching and preparation have been, that pupils will not turn the drama into an
   amusing skit. The important point here is to avoid a situation in which this

approach to drama becomes the norm. There may need to be a specific discussion with the class about styles and appropriate genres. Better still, observation of the work of another class through performance or video may be enough to raise expectations. The preoccupation with self-expression and creativity tended to result in the avoidance of using models of other drama for fear of overly derivative work, but the result is usually to motivate classes rather than have them simply copy the work of others. Alternatively, it may be appropriate to bring variety so that pupils are given text to work on next lesson or are invited deliberately to work on comedy.

6 Sometimes a class are unable to hold a tableau without giggling. In this case it may be helpful to take them back to some basic exercises of freezing, holding a freeze frame in pairs, etc. Attitude to drama is determined not just by the experience of the class but by their mood on a particular day – sensitivity to that fact is needed.

7 If the drama work becomes rather too exuberant and physical the teacher can ask the class to freeze, break into a narrative and pause to invite groups to take up the events briefly before the narrative is resumed.

It was suggested at the beginning of this chapter that the discrete use of conventions can detract from the process of play-making which is at the heart of engagement in drama. However, as pupils become more experienced in drama they can be expected to acquire the ability themselves to use conventions deliberately when asked to prepare and present plays. For example, the drama of younger classes can be greatly facilitated by the use of narrative, a convention with which they may be familiar from the experience of the part of the narrator in scripted plays. Conventions such as the creation of action off-stage, scene divisions, dealing with expositions and endings, direct address to the audience, and various Brechtian techniques such as speaking stage directions or speaking in the third person, can be acquired and experienced through approaches to text, which is the subject of the next chapter.

Further reading

Neelands, J. (1990a) *Structuring Drama Work* (edited by T. Goode) contains a very comprehensive guide to conventions and techniques used in drama teaching. See also Barlow, S. and Skidmore, S. (1994) *Dramaform*, McGuire, B. (1998) *Student Handbook for Drama*, Marson *et al.* (1990) *Drama 14–16*. Readers interested in further work on still image might turn to Boal, A. (1992) *Games for Actors and Non-Actors* and an article by Eriksson and Jantzen (1992). The key book on mantle of the expert is Heathcote, D. and Bolton, G. (1994) *Drama for Learning: An Account of Dorothy Heathcote's 'Mantle of the Expert'*. For articles dealing with this approach see Hill (1991), Bryer (1990). The concept of teacher in role is dealt with at various times in Johnson, L. and O'Neill, C. (1984) *Dorothy Heathcote: Collected Writings on Education and Drama*; see also Carey (1990).

Approaches to text

Working with script

THERE HAS BEEN a long tradition in drama teaching of seeing 'improvisation' and 'working from script' as two very different activities often associated with the different 'drama' and 'theatre' traditions described in Chapter 2. However, as indicated in Chapter 5, much of the work which was described as 'improvisation' was not spontaneous but usually planned and devised drama which could be repeated. Thus categories such as 'planned' and 'polished' improvisation emerged which invites a line of argument as follows. When 'improvisations' are repeated they need to be short enough to be memorised, at least in broad outline. If the improvisation is short enough to be repeated then this is much the same as working from a script, even though nothing is written down. It might be argued that when an improvisation is repeated it is never *exactly* the same but of course that it also true of work from script which accounts for the appeal of live performance. Traditional distinctions therefore are once again not as clear cut as is often assumed.

This chapter will be concerned with possible approaches to scripted plays in the classroom as well as the use of different texts as a basis for drama. It is common to use the term 'text' in the context of drama to refer not just to the printed word on the page but to any sign system which can be the object of interpretation (including media text and improvisation). The use of the word 'text' here in the more traditional sense is simply for convenience to include written plays as well as other useful sources such as poetry and prose. Although the work on play texts and poetry is likely to be more relevant to the English and drama specialist, the work on prose is likely to be of interest to teachers of all subjects.

One of the criticisms levelled at the drama in education tradition has been the lack of attention to scripted drama and the excessive domination of lessons by various forms of improvisation (Hornbrook 1991). It is certainly true, judging by the literature of the last three decades, that script has not been a central focus in drama, but there has never been outright hostility to play texts as such. Slade (1954) saw script as coming at the end of a developmental process at approximately 14 years. Alington (1961) made a contrast between 'creation' involved in improvisation and what he called 'creation-interpretation' involved in work on scripted plays. Heathcote (1984: 89) recognised that some teachers worked better with script and non-verbal modes but also argued that working with text is likely to be more suitable for the young adult of 17 than the child of 7. This developmental perspective which saw work on text as coming at a late stage in a pupil's school career was one of the reasons for the neglect of play scripts. Other reasons ranged from theoretical considerations (drama's association with theories of self-expression and traditional literary assumptions about what reading a script involves) to those which are more practical (conventions of curriculum organisation and accessibility of texts to pupils). These need to be considered in more detail.

Creativity and self-expression

The emphasis on 'creativity' in drama meant that working from text tended to be seen as an inferior form of activity, involving as it did someone else's second-hand ideas rather than one's own. Similarly, the emphasis on self-expression emphasised spontaneous drama of pupils' own making rather than the process of giving utterance to other people's writing. Implicit in this view was the notion that responding to the written word was not in itself a creative act, an idea which was challenged by later thinking, including in particular reader-response theories. If we add to those contemporary arguments Derrida's challenging notion that writing is in some ways more 'fundamental' than speech, that it may give a more faithful insight into language and meaning than our intuitive thinking about the spoken word, the argument against script become even weaker (Fleming 2001: 92). As indicated in Chapter 5, Slade's notion of Child Drama was based on the observation of the natural activity of children at play and the role of the teacher was to nurture rather than intervene; the emphasis was on dramatic playing rather than what was seen as work on static, received ideas of others contained in drama texts. There is no reason, however, why work on script should not be as creative and engaging as other activities.

Relationship between drama and English in the curriculum

Another reason for the neglect of play text in drama was that it was largely seen as the province of the English curriculum. As indicated in Chapter 2, plays were studied as 'literature' rather than as 'drama' *per se*. In practice, in many schools this meant reading around the class prior to studying the text with emphasis on character, motivation and language rather than the semiotics of performance. Prose, poetry and drama have been traditionally the three genres studied for public examinations, and that influence has been felt throughout the English curriculum. Text has been absent from the drama lesson partly then because of an implicit assumption that it is in English lessons that the study of drama as subject occurs and what was meant by 'study' in that context was largely based on literary analysis derived from the tradition of new criticism.

Traditional literary assumptions

A third reason for the neglect of scripted drama is derived from traditional views of what it means to read or perform a play. Reading and interpretation were seen as essentially passive activities performed on texts with static meanings as opposed to the more creative practice of improvised drama. The influence of literary theory, however, has changed the notion of what reading and response in drama entails: 'meaning' is more fruitfully seen not as residing in the text according to the intention of the author but as a function of the active meaning-bestowing activity of the reader. Such theoretical perspectives have important implications for the types of practical activities possible with texts which go far beyond simply the acting out of an extract according to the intentions of the author.

Difficulties involved in performing play text

Another more practical reason for the neglect of text has been the recognition that the performance of scripted work demands more developed skills than the more accessible improvised play-making. Inevitably teachers asked themselves whether it was worth all the effort of having pupils learn lines in order to be able to engage in anything resembling a reasonable performance of a play. Unless pupils learn lines traditional work on script becomes little more than play-reading. Nor was it an insignificant point that work on scripted drama was more difficult for pupils with limited reading ability who could flourish in lessons dominated by improvisation.

Quality of plays written for pupils

Watkins (1981) commented on the lack of suitable scripted plays for children and observed that high quality literary material for children is rather to be found in prose and poetry. There have been more texts published since then but a similar point was made by Burgess and Gaudry in 1985 when they pointed out that much of the material available was inappropriate, with play scripts being too long or of poor quality. Certainly many of the plays which have been written specifically for schools tend to work too hard to appeal to what are seen to be the interests of young people and often lack depth.

Approaches to script

Implicit in the criticism that there is a dearth of texts available which are both of high quality and accessible is the idea that play texts must inevitably be acted and, moreover, performed in their entirety. Once one is liberated from that notion it is possible to work on quite demanding texts in more limited ways. This assumption also underlies some of the other reasons identified for the neglect of play scripts. Just as at one time it was traditionally assumed in drama in education that improvised work should never involve performance, the assumption seems to have been that work on script should always involve the acting of entire plays. However, there are many practical workshop activities on extracts which can be used to encourage pupils to a deeper understanding of the way scripts work as drama and can provide a foundation for more extended work on play production. They also provide a means of focusing specifically on response to drama. The following activities can be used with extracts from different works or from one central text. They can be used in combination with one another, working progressively from simple exercises to more demanding activities and can lead to more ambitious projects on play texts.

- Select an extract from a play, delete the characters' names and ask groups to use clues in the text to decide how many characters, who they are, and what the context might be. This activity allows pupils to become familiar with a particular text extract but also encourages them to think about meaning and the way meaning is determined by context. By using extracts from different periods pupils can be alerted to differences of language and style. It is useful to choose an extract which allows for differences of interpretation. However, it is worth pointing out that it is customary for pupils to view this exercise as one which requires them to guess the right answer, rather than encouraging a free play of imagination over the chosen extract. As such it is in danger of being counter-productive if it carries the implicit message that the exercise is an unreasonable test which denies the pupils the information which would allow them to supply the right answer. A preliminary exercise, therefore, which uses chosen lines which do not have a pre-determined meaning, can introduce the notion that the purpose is not to guess the right context (for in this case it does not exist) but to think up situations which fit the dialogue. The challenge is to determine different contexts and for the class as a whole to decide which draws more successfully on the extract. A very simple exchange such as the following can be used to introduce the idea:

It's all right, I came back.
Did you get it?
Keep your voice down.
Nothing happened.
Is it there?
I said nothing happened.

- A scripted exchange of a few lines between two people can be given to groups of four pupils who are then asked to supply the actual thoughts of the characters which are not spoken. This exercise introduces pupils to the notion of subtext and the essential idea that the meaning of an utterance is more complex than the surface meaning of the words. The exchange can be 'performed' with two pupils reading the dialogue and two others following each utterance with the real thoughts. Once again, it is helpful to introduce the idea with a simple exchange as in the following example:

Would you like to collect it now?
It's rather late but okay, I'll come in just for a minute.
Of course it might take me a while to find it.
That's no problem, I'll give you a hand and it won't take long.
You know perhaps we should leave it until tomorrow.

- A variation on the idea is to use a small extract of dialogue in the same way but this time ask for the intended meaning of the speaker which may or may not be different from the surface meaning of the words spoken.

I really like that scarf you're wearing. (What an ugly scarf)
Thank you very much. (Don't be so insulting)
It must have cost a fortune. (It looks cheap)

This activity can highlight the way in which a change in tone is needed to convey the underlying meaning of the words.

- The meaning of an extract can also be changed by varying the actions or gestures which accompany the words spoken. A simple extract can be used to introduce the exercise – e.g. 'If you don't leave now you are going to be late.' How might the actions of the speaker (as opposed to just tone) change to convey indifference, anxiety, authority (e.g. speaker may be reading a paper, advancing towards the other person, gesticulating)?

- A longer extract may be enacted in different ways to convey different meanings through a combination of tone/gesture etc. These activities are best conducted with very little emphasis on sharing work. It can be more embarrassing and inhibiting trying to share work of this nature than it is to perform improvised pieces.

- Groups can be asked to create a tableau of a specific point in the play (e.g. end of a scene). Where (etc.) would the characters/actors be on stage in relation to each other and what feelings would they be portraying? This workshop activity can be employed in the course of reading a play. It asks the pupils to focus attention on stage design and on the sign system which accompanies the actual recital of the words of the text to convey meaning.

- Groups can be asked to work out actors'/directors' notes about movement, tone, positions, etc. for a given script extract. Pupils find it helpful to be given a completed example to demonstrate what is required. This is a more difficult exercise than is sometimes thought and pupils need a knowledge of the play as a whole as it is difficult to work on an extract out of context. Care needs to be taken to avoid having pupils turn this into a paper exercise; they should be encouraged to experiment practically with their ideas.

- A related task is to ask pupils to identify the implicit stage directions in the script extract.

- By asking pupils to read part of a script from a play and continue in improvised form they are being encouraged to be active in their reading through anticipation and prediction. This exercise also asks pupils to test out their understanding of character and meaning and can serve as a means of introducing the next section of text for study.

- Groups can be asked to improvise scenes which were not shown in the play – e.g. meetings between characters, scenes prior to the start of the play, etc. Underlying this activity is a dynamic rather than static view of the meaning of the text as a whole.

- Attention to the art of condensing meaning into a few words can be focused by asking pupils to prepare a simple scene on a given topic by using as few as seven words.

- A rather more demanding activity is to ask a class to reduce a section of a play to its essence and perform it – e.g. the opening scene of *King Lear*. It is best done by making a specific requirement of words, e.g. eight lines. As with some of the other activities listed here, the words can be memorised with little effort.

- Act out a simple exchange of dialogue and then use the same dialogue in different contexts (e.g. prison, old people's home, on telephone) with very different meanings. Again, like some of the other activities listed here the aim is to sensitise pupils to the degree to which meaning is not determined by the words on the page but arises from the total context. Once again, preliminary exercises with short exchanges can be used first to introduce the idea.

How is Mary getting on?
She's doing okay.
It's so long since I've seen her.
She misses you, you know.
Tell her I received her letter.

- Act out the same piece of dialogue trying to show (a) a close relationship between the two characters, then (b) a distant relationship, (c) different status between the two characters.

- Take a moment of dialogue from a play and ask all other characters present to speak aloud their thoughts at that moment.

- A more advanced activity is to provide groups with lines of dialogue and ask them to create two contexts. One of these uses the words in a straightforward way, the other has an ironic meaning. For example, the line 'It is really good to be here' has more impact when the audience knows the speaker is about to be killed.

Script writing

Script writing has an important place in both the English and drama lesson.

Writing plays in the English classroom is sometimes viewed as just another activity aimed at developing pupils' writing rather than a method of furthering pupils' understanding of drama. It is easy to see script writing as simply a way of recording speech (an alternative to speech marks) without placing enough focus on conscious crafting and shaping. As with work on play texts, it is not always necessary to think in terms of complete works; it is often enough to work with short extracts. As illustrated in Chapter 1 in relation to the Pied Piper, work on script can blend with what might have been described in the past as more process-oriented activities. The following list provides examples of content which pupils can be taught in relation to script writing:

- conventions related to setting out a script and the way these have changed;

- ways of conveying important background information to an audience;

- the way lines of dialogue can convey implicit stage directions;

- differences between written dialogue and speech in narrative;

- differences which can often be identified between script and everyday speech;

- ways of conveying a character's thoughts through dialogue and actions;

- using pauses to change the mood;

- creating effects through very short and more extended exchanges;

- structural devices used by playwrights (e.g. non-linear plots);

- conveying character through style of speech.

Shakespeare in schools

Active approaches to Shakespeare draw on techniques derived from drama and literature teaching, theatre and voice training to make texts enjoyable and accessible to pupils of all ages and abilities. Because the aim and the focus of the work is clear and unquestioned, there is very little of the agonising which has been characteristic of drama in education in past years over what counts as 'drama' or whether particular methodologies are acceptable. Critics of the approach who argue that there is much more to the study of Shakespeare than the practical approaches advocated in the project can easily be answered by the simple observation that these activities are designed to complement rather than be a substitute for more traditional methods.

It is not the intention in this section to describe in great detail the variety of activities advocated by the Shakespeare and Schools project, accounts of which can be found in the titles given in the further reading section at the end of this chapter. It may be helpful, however, to consider the way in which some of the broad principles underlying the work can enhance an understanding of drama teaching in general.

Many of the activities on Shakespeare can be said to work from the 'outside' in that one of the central aims is to have the pupils become comfortable and familiar with the language of the plays and respond to its rhythms and images prior to any detailed attempt at understanding and analysis of its content. An example of a simple workshop approach to a Shakespeare text might involve the following steps:

1 The class engage in a number of warm-up games and exercises of the kind described in Chapter 4.

2 Lines from a speech (or extracts from the play on a particular theme) are distributed so that individuals have only one small section which they will need to memorise and repeat.

3 The class are given various individual activities designed to familiarise individuals with their line (vocalise words to actions, whisper, speak quickly, slowly).

4 Groups are given further activities designed to familiarise them further with the text (e.g. going through the motions of an argument using the words of the play).

5 The class then reconstruct the speech in order, so that each individual has only a small section to repeat. Sound, music and possibly action may be added.

Because the work has a clear external objective and a script it is possible to focus less specifically on the meaning of the content in a way which would not be possible with spontaneous improvisation for in the latter case the subject matter of the drama needs to be clear to the participants. Thus the teaching methods can be used in a rather more mechanical way than is often possible in a drama which needs to be negotiated with the participants. The techniques not only make Shakespeare accessible to pupils but provide teachers with relatively safe structures which can be undertaken with classes.

Another aspect of this work is that it reinforces the idea advocated in Chapter 4 that classroom exercises have to be judged not in isolation but in particular contexts. Voice exercises tend to be associated in some people's minds with mindless attention to form with no focus at all on content. Yet many exercises which are designed to relax participants physically and to enhance vocalisation may have their place in a wider context of work on text. The balance is a delicate one – external exercises can usefully be introduced during a project or session rather than necessarily as the starting point for work because pupils need to have a sense of purpose in what they are doing. Rodenburg (1993) describes warm-up exercises (preparing the body, voice and speech muscles), language exercises (storytelling, describing objects, epic storytelling), sounding words (whispering, chanting the text, speaking the words while moving, vocalising the first and last words of lines, isolating verbs and nouns, voicing the vowels) which all can make useful contributions to work on text. Because these activities are intended to familiarise pupils with the rhythm of the verse they are also valuable approaches to work on poetry.

Other approaches to Shakespeare can include some of the examples of activities given in earlier chapters:

- use of tableaux to get pupils to think about use of space, physical gesture when particular lines are spoken;

- use of choral reading for speeches;

- questioning particular characters in role to uncover attitude and motivation;

- questioning very minor characters in role (e.g. a servant) to reinforce knowledge of the plot;

- voicing a character's thoughts aloud at a moment of dilemma and decision-making;

- creating mime to accompany a sequence of text to draw attention to details of language.

Drama and poetry

Work which combines these two genres can be valuable for both English teachers and specialists in drama. From the English teacher's point of view the use of drama to teach poetry can be valuable because, as with the approach to Shakespeare described above, familiarity with the text and personal response can be encouraged without necessarily resorting to premature cognitive comprehension and analysis; one of the challenges facing teachers of poetry is how to encourage and legitimise personal response and active reading without resorting to received meanings. From the drama teacher's point of view a poem can provide an objective 'script' and new starting point for the lesson which gives a fresh impetus to familiar themes.

Many of the techniques for individual and choral reading used by the Shakespeare in Schools project can also be employed for poetry. In the examples which follow, however, the challenge for the groups involved was to move more clearly from one genre to another by taking a poem and representing it as a short 'play'. Work of this kind is best undertaken with groups who have some experience in drama and initially with poems which lend themselves more easily to dramatic interpretation. That does not mean that they all necessarily have to have a strong narrative base, but poems which have a thematic rather than purely descriptive content and which invite interpretation are more suitable for this kind of work.

For the examples which follow, the sessions began with warm-up role play exercises (see Chapter 4). The work on poetic text can be introduced by basing the final role play exercise on a single line – e.g. 'Telling lies to the young is wrong' – and asking the pupils not to present an elaborate story but to enact a simple situation which might accompany the line. If the teacher has previously video-recorded pupils working from poetry, this can also be a very helpful means of demonstrating the requirements of the project and provides motivation for forming a 'contract' with the class that they will accept the challenge of working in groups on whatever poem they are given. This approach avoids a crude imposition of poem on the pupils without respecting their capacity for independent choice, but also avoids taking an inordinate amount of time while the groups themselves make a choice. One of the objectives of the project is for the pupils to explore possibilities of translating from one genre to another in ways which might not at first seem obvious to them. The teacher's role is to support them in their efforts but not to rob them of their own interpretations. While reader-response theories have emphasised the centrality of the reader's role in the making of meaning, it is important not to leave pupils struggling with difficult texts in a way which might leave them alienated or bored. A failure to understand some aspects of syntax and vocabulary can provide insurmountable barriers. It is better to opt for more accessible poems which are easily unpacked in the early stages of this work; more difficult poems can be introduced not so much when it is thought that pupils will understand them but when they are likely to feel empowered to experiment with meaning. By working in this way they should develop at least a tacit grasp of the fact that full cognitive comprehension is not required for meaningful response in dramatic form because poetry does not yield the same sorts of meanings as other types of written discourse. In the examples which follow, the pupils were reminded that they did not have to develop an elaborate plot but they did have to incorporate a reading of the poem somewhere into their work. The decision whether to present the work or not could be made at the end.

First Ice

by Andrei Voznesensky

A girl freezes in a telephone booth.
In her draughty overcoat she hides
a face all smeared
In tears and lipstick.

She breathes on her thin palms.
Her fingers are icy. She wears earrings.
She'll have to go home alone, alone,
Along the icy street.

First ice. It is the first time.
The first ice of telephone phrases.
Frozen tears glitter on her cheeks –
The first ice of human hurt.

This poem is usually interpreted as having adolescent love as its theme. It was interesting therefore that a Year 10 group based their drama on the relationship between a mother and teenage daughter. The finished work was very simple, incorporated two scenes and lasted no more than four minutes. The alienation of mother and daughter was demonstrated in a simple, restrained sequence in which the girl returned from school with her younger sister and was subtly 'frozen out' by the mother, symbolised by the latter's preoccupation with the younger girl's drawing (which eventually got crumpled) and demonstrated more explicitly by her indifferent response to the daughter's gentle plea, 'Mum, are you listening, I've got something to tell you.' The second scene was situated at a telephone booth where, after being awkwardly comforted by someone else waiting for the telephone, the teenage girl, attempting to hold back tears, phones 'child-line'. The drama is held as still image while the poem is read, 'A girl freezes in a telephone booth . . .' The group have not just responded to content because the style of their drama (stark, understated, condensed) replicates that of the poem. Although they have provided more of a context than the original work, their version is similar to it in that they make no attempt to supply every detail: as observers of the drama we are invited to speculate on the precise cause of the difficulty but we are left in no doubt as to the emotional impact on the girl. The pupils have made their response to the poem without over-emphasising either the text or the reader. They have needed to become extremely familiar with the work without being forced prematurely into analysis.

My Parents Kept Me From Children Who Were Rough

by Stephen Spender

My parents kept me from children who were rough
Who threw words like stones and who wore torn clothes.
Their thighs showed through rags. They ran in the street
And climbed cliffs and stripped by country streams.

I feared more than tigers their muscles like iron
Their jerking hands and their knees tight on my arms.
I feared the salt coarse pointing of those boys
Who copied my lisp behind me on the road.

They were lithe, they sprang out behind hedges
Like dogs to bark at my world. They threw mud
While I looked the other way, pretending to smile.
I longed to forgive them, but they never smiled.

The group who worked on this poem, as might be expected from the content, produced work with a stronger narrative thrust but did not fall into the trap of attempting to tell a complete story. The way they 'de-familiarised' the poem was to cast a girl as the narrator. The strong physicality of the 'rough boys' which is conveyed by the animal imagery in the poem was symbolised in the drama by the playing of a game (which had figured in the earlier warm-up) in which the participants grasp each other's hands while standing around a chair and try to pull each other in to touch it; the loser is the first one to touch the chair. The outsider in the drama was presented as being too timid to play the game effectively and watches enviously as the others demonstrate how it is done. The rest of the drama focused on the girl's family and their objections to her mixing with these children but revealing that their concern is primarily with their own social standing with the neighbours. In this example the poem was given a group reading before the presentation of the drama.

What Has Happened to Lulu?

by Charles Causley

What has happened to Lulu, mother?
What has happened to Lu?
There's nothing in her bed but an old rag doll
And by its side a shoe.

Why is her window wide, mother,
The curtain flapping free,
And only a circle on the dusty shelf
Where her money-box used to be?

Why do you turn your head, mother,
And why do the tear-drops fall?
And why do you crumple that note on the fire
And say it is nothing at all?

I woke to voices late last night,
I heard an engine roar.
Why do you tell me the things I heard
Were a dream and nothing more?

I heard somebody cry, mother,
In anger or in pain,
But now I ask you why, mother,
You say it was a gust of rain.

Why do you wander about as though
You don't know what to do?
What has happened to Lulu, mother?
What has happened to Lu?

In each example, the preparation of the reading and the decision about where it should come in relation to the drama were important aspects of the project as a whole and contributed to the final meaning of the work. In this case the drama came between a reading of verses, with the very last line given to the mother. The group provided a context which is not given in the poem (Lulu has gone off to live with her estranged father) but stayed faithful to the form of the poem by having the refrain, which is also the title, central. The events are seen through the eyes of a younger sister who is shown in the drama lying in bed listening to the voices downstairs (using conventions described in Chapter 6).

The Bully Asleep

by John Walsh

This afternoon, when grassy
Scents through the classroom crept,
Bill Craddock laid his head
Down on his desk, and slept.

The children came round him:
Jimmy, Roger, and Jane;
They lifted his head timidly
And let it sink again.

'Look, he's gone sound asleep, Miss,'
Said Jimmy Adair;
'He stays up all the night, you see;
His mother doesn't care.'

'Stand away from him children.'
Miss Andrews stopped to see.
'Yes, he's asleep; go on
With your writing, and let him be.'

'Now's a good chance!' whispered Jimmy;
And he snatched Bill's pen and hid it.
'Kick him under the desk, hard;
He won't know who did it.'

'Fill all his pockets with rubbish –
Paper, apple-cores, chalk.'
So they plotted, while Jane
Sat wide-eyed at their talk.

Not caring, not hearing,
Bill Craddock he slept on;
Lips parted, eyes closed –
Their cruelty gone.

'Stick him with pins!' muttered Roger.
'Ink down his neck!' said Jim.
But Jane, tearful and foolish,
Wanted to comfort him.

This poem has less ambiguity and lends itself to a more straightforward interpretation to drama. A Year 7 group focused on what they saw as the crucial element of the poem – the sympathy Jane felt for the bully – and presented a scene before the events of the poem in which she is seen living next door to the boy and therefore aware of his difficulties: she can overhear the problems in his household. The classroom scene was presented much as described in the poem but interestingly the group attempted to incorporate the descriptive elements in the first few lines, which set the scene into the dramatic presentation.

Drama and prose

As suggested above, combining work on poetry and drama can be valuable for both teachers of drama and English. The nature of the emphasis will vary in that the latter are likely to want to take advantage of the degree of familiarity with the work and the element of personal response provided by the drama to proceed to closer analysis of form and poetic technique. Prose extracts can likewise provide a fresh stimulus and focus for drama, while for teachers of other subjects the meaning of texts can be opened up in new ways.

There has been a considerable amount of interesting work on drama and narrative since the early 1980s. Writers have shown how drama work can go beyond a mere enactment of the events of the narrative to explore multiple viewpoints, expand the events of the story and animate the original text for the reader. Many of the techniques used can also be employed to explore non-fiction. 'Comprehension' as an exercise has tended to mean asking pupils questions, often of a closed or literal kind. However, it is generally speaking the tasks in which pupils are asked to engage, rather than the questions posed, which invite them to gain possession of the texts presented to them, be they short stories, newspaper articles, historical documents, letters or scripts.

The advantage of working with script in drama is that it exists as an external reference point which demands work which need be no less creative or original than totally free improvisation. This is because pupils are not trying to replicate the intention of the author but are being offered a 'free-play' around the text to interpret and develop their understanding. Similarly, a prose extract whether fictional or non-fictional can be used within the drama as a focus for planning the work. Techniques such as questioning in role, tableau, documentary, pairs work can be applied to particular written passages in the context of drama as a starting point for the lesson, and in the context of other subjects to develop understanding of the subject.

Even unlikely sources can be explored through drama techniques. The following extract is from a book written in 1575 by a Dutch visitor to London.

> Wives in England are entirely in the power of their husbands, yet they are not kept so strictly as in Spain. Nor are they shut up. . . . They go to market to buy what they like best to eat. They are well-dressed, fond of taking it easy and leave the care of the household to their STEWARDS. They sit in front of their doors, dressed in fine clothes, to see and be seen by passers by. In all banquets and feasts they are shown the highest honour . . . All the rest of the time they spend in walking and riding, in playing at cards, in visiting their friends, conversing with their neighbours and making merry with them and childbirths and christenings. And all this with the permission of their husbands. This is why England is called the paradise of married women.
>
> (Adapted from Culpin (1992) and reprinted in NCC (1993: 73))

How might drama techniques be used to make the text more accessible to pupils? The author could be questioned in role to establish more details about his visit to England. Pupils could be asked to create different tableaux showing some of the scenes which he saw which made him draw these conclusions. They then voice the thoughts of the characters involved which, had he been aware of them, might have made him temper his views. A pairs exercise might show the author meeting with another traveller who had also visited England but who had come to a different conclusion, although he had witnessed many of the same scenes. A second meeting takes place with someone who had seen very different scenes of poverty and deprivation. In groups the class could be asked to script and enact a scene from the present day, ironically entitled 'England, the paradise of married women'. The drama is used to introduce and explore questions on the interpretation of historical sources.

Further reading

For ideas on working with scripts see Kempe, A. (1988) *The Drama Sampler*, Kempe, A. and Warner, L. (1997) *Starting with Scripts*, Nicholson, H. (2000) *Teaching Drama 11–18*, Shiach, D. (1987) *Front Page to Performance*. For books on Shakespeare in schools see Reynolds, P. (1991) *Practical Approaches to Teaching Shakespeare*, Gibson, R. (1990) *Secondary School Shakespeare*. The journal *Shakespeare and Schools* (Cambridge Institute of Education) is a valuable source of practical ideas. Detailed work on text is described in Berry, C. (1993) *The Actor and the Text* (revised edition). For articles which deal with drama and narrative see Booth (1989) and Byron (1984).

CHAPTER

8

Performing and responding

Performance drama

ONE OF THE ARGUMENTS of this book is that there is no correct or incorrect way of classifying drama activities. It is important, however, to understand the consequences of particular forms of categorisation whether these were originally intended or not. As outlined in Chapter 1, the development of thinking about drama teaching can be described in terms of the way distinctions between terms such as 'theatre' and 'drama', 'process' and 'product' have been eroded. It is likewise difficult to defend an exclusive distinction between modes of drama which are oriented towards performance of some kind and drama which exists solely for the sake of the participants. It was suggested in the introduction to this book that a more meaningful distinction can be made between forms of 'dramatic playing' and 'drama as an art form' which embraces 'process' drama and theatre performances. A concept of signification (with its embedded notion of negotiating and sharing meaning) is central to drama activity irrespective of the degree to which communication to an audience is the central goal. However, it is possible to distinguish those drama projects which specifically culminate in performance from drama which has not had communication to an external audience as one of its central objectives. It is likely that some projects will start as classroom improvised dramas but may be developed later and polished for sharing with an audience. It was a matter of some contention among writers in drama teaching whether there is any significant difference in the nature of the work when oriented specifically towards performance and the degree to which such work should figure in drama lessons. Hornbrook's comment (1998a: 104) – 'It is my contention that conceptually there is nothing which differentiates the child acting in the classroom from the actor on the stage of the theatre' – has been specifically challenged by Bolton (1990: 5):

> Now this is where Hornbrook and I differ fundamentally because stand point seriously affects the structuring of the drama, pupil/teacher expectations of the outcome and subsequent reflection and evaluation. At a philosophical level one could agree with Hornbrook's argument that dramatic activity is always a performance because even the

child in solitary play is an audience to him/herself – just as in 'real life' one is an observer of one's solitary actions. The conclusion would have to be therefore that all activity is of the same kind, a bizarre conclusion, which however logically sound in terms of audience awareness is not in the least bit useful to anyone.

It should be noticed that the difference of opinion is not about whether there is some place for performance drama in schools but the degree to which performance should be considered central. The key question is whether having pupils present work to an audience changes the nature of the drama experience and hence the potential educational objectives. In order to understand the difference of emphasis it is helpful to examine why there has been hostility within the tradition of drama in education to asking children to perform.

The negative aspects of the traditional school play have been stated clearly by Allen (1979: 128), even though he was one of the writers who have consistently argued against the denigration of performance. He describes the typical nativity play as follows:

> The occasion usually involves a fairly large number of children, dressing-up, lines learnt, scenery shakily erected, and as large an audience as the hall will hold. In performance we have inaudibility, lack of involvement, angel's eyes searching for Nan in the audience and friendly smiles when contact is made – every kind of distortion that destroys the very nature of the performance that is being offered.

Lack of authenticity or attention to content, the cultivation of spoiled child stars, the investment of inordinate amounts of time for little return were all deemed to be negative aspects of school productions. Slade (1954: 351) likewise was very concerned that consciousness of an audience would destroy the sincerity of the drama work and produce show-offs, or, using his colourful terminology, 'bombastic little boasters'. Performance on stage has had negative associations for many writers and practitioners. O'Neill and Lambert (1982: 25) commented that performance could result in a 'superficial playing out of events, lacking in seriousness and sometimes accompanied by a certain degree of showing off'.

A common criticism of the school play was that it was of more benefit to the reputation of the school than to the participants. A more accommodating view recognised that involvement in school productions brought many positive outcomes, including the generation of a community ethos and cross-curricular cooperation, but still questioned the educational potential of the work as drama. 'Acting' was judged to involve the artificial imitation of emotion rather than the experiencing of 'real' feeling. Performing on stage was not thought to offer the same rich experience which could be had in a drama workshop. As with the argument against the use of text, it could be claimed that views of this kind were largely based on a narrow model of theatre practice and of the actors' and director's role, assuming, for example, that pupils would be mere automatons in the control of the teacher/director. Moreover, asking pupils to act was thought to be equivalent to asking them to show off, rather than assuming that 'showing off' was simply a case of bad acting.

The term 'acting' has tended to be avoided in drama in education because of the implied preoccupation with communication rather than with experiencing or exploration. However, the assumption that an actor on stage is primarily concerned with communication to an audience is an over-simplification of what is actually happening. Apart from instances of monologues, soliloquies and other forms of direct address to the audience, the primary act of communication is not between actor and audience but between actor and fellow actor in role (Elam 1980: 38).

The traditional dismissal of acting as being inappropriate for drama in education did not always take into account the potential diversity of the concept of 'acting'. The nature of the experience and feeling of the participants has been as much subject to debate in the context of acting and theatre practice as it has been in drama in education. A central dichotomy in both has traditionally centred on 'emotion' versus 'technique', the question being whether the primary emphasis should be placed on 'externals' such as gesture or 'inner processes' and feelings (Harrop 1992).

States (1985: 163) in his *Great Reckonings in Little Rooms*, has suggested that there are three major acting modes (as distinct from styles) or ways in which the actor's relationship to the audience can change. He describes these in terms which relate them to the pronominals 'I', 'you' and 'he':

I (actor) = Self-expressive mode
You (audience) = Collaborative mode
He (character) = Representational mode

In self-expressive mode the actor seems to be projecting himself, drawing attention to his craft, saying in effect 'see what I can do'. States describes opera, dance and mime as the major self-expressive forms of theatre because what they are about is always less important than what they display: 'The best-known example is the opera soprano who is not expected to disappear into her role as a dying tubercular, because it is impossible to sing properly and die properly at the same time.' In the collaborative mode the equivalent of some form of 'you' address is used in relation to the audience (either explicitly or implicitly). The distance between actor and audience is broken down and the latter is given a more active role. 'In general, this mode may be symbolized by the comic aside which presumes that the audience is in complicity with the settings of traps or deceits – or to put it another way, the actor plays a character who lives in a world that includes the audience' (*ibid.*: 170). In the representational mode of performance the actor's energy is focused not on displaying his own art (the self-expressive mode) or on communicating with the audience in the collaborative sense described above but he appears to be bent on 'becoming' his or her character. The representational mode derives from the idea that we come to the theatre to see a *play*, 'an enactment of significant human experience', rather than a *performance* (*ibid.*: 181).

This has necessarily been a brief summary of a complex analysis but it is possible to see the rejection of a concept of 'acting' in drama teaching as being more accurately described as a rejection of self-presentation in favour of representational modes, although this has been presented as a rejection of acting *per se*. 'Acting' tends to be used as a term with one precise meaning but in fact may be classified according to the demands of a particular genre (farce or melodrama), historical period or particular school. The contrast found in the work of Brecht and Stanislavski figures quite significantly in writing on drama teaching. The changes in the latter's thinking and practice through his career represent a search for a methodology which would result in the effective merging of the actor's self and character in the part. An aspect of Brecht's theatre and part of the radicalising intention of alienation was to retain the very gulf between the actor and role which Stanislavski had been concerned to eliminate.

Suspicion of the term 'acting' in the context of school work in drama belongs to an era which rejected inauthentic imitation of behaviour ('show me a happy boy, now a sad boy') in favour of more genuine feeling. There was also concern to emphasise the difference between drama which would specifically culminate in performance (with its need for repeatability and more technical sophistication) and drama which is enacted for its own sake. However, the use of the term 'acting' is a helpful reminder that spontaneous improvised drama in the studio resembles more closely performance on the stage than it does real life; central to the art form is the recognition that drama operates in a fictitious mode. If participants actually believe in the situation, either because they have been deceived or because they have become too involved, it ceases to be drama. It also recognises that within the tradition of theatre there have been different interpretations of what acting should involve, different styles and modes. One way of describing the development of drama in education is to see it as making a contribution to acting and theatre methodology. Bennett (1990: 1) has pointed out that 'Conventional notions of theatre and of theatre audiences too often rely on the model of the commercial mainstream' which in the context of this discussion could be described as self-expressive acting, passive audiences, authoritative directors. Rehearsal methods for the school play are likely to be different in a school which has a strong tradition of drama in education, as will be seen in the final section of this chapter.

When drama work is oriented towards performance to an external audience it is fairly clear that some priorities will change. This can lead to superficiality (as so many of the early writers on drama teaching recognised) but that is by no means a necessary consequence. The distinction between 'making' and 'performing' which is found in most of the published attainment targets for drama is in danger of preserving some traditional views: that it is in the context of 'making' that pupils are being creative, exploratory and imaginative whereas when performing they are only focusing on technical skills. Conversely it may imply that when pupils are 'making' they are not oriented towards performance.

Responding

At the height of the drama/theatre divide described in Chapter 1, teaching pupils how to respond to drama was not given very much attention because the emphasis was more on creativity and self-expression. Responding is now generally recognised as an important aim in drama teaching but it is not always recognised that it is important to get a balance between an *authentic* and *informed* response. For pupils to be able to respond to drama (their own and that of others) they need frameworks and structures within which to operate. On the other hand it is important that technical jargon does not become a substitute for personal response which derives from genuine engagement. Several writers listed in the further reading section at the end of this chapter have provided lists of the factors which should be taken into account when 'reading' a performance (e.g. words, delivery of the text, facial expression, gesture, movement, make-up, hairstyle, costume, props, sets, lighting, music, sound-effects, framing devices) but these need to be used in a way which is not unduly mechanistic.

Meaning in drama is not merely a function of the 'objective', formal qualities of the sign system. It is not enough for pupils to be able to talk about the technical aspects of a play (scenery, acting and lighting, etc.) unless they can relate their insights to the content. This suggests that the starting point for responding to a play should be the work itself and what makes it distinctive rather than a predetermined list of characteristics imposed on every play. The immediate reactions of pupils to a drama whether in the classroom or theatre should be the starting point for more systematic explanations.

A useful way of achieving the balance being recommended here is not to see responding simply as a cognitive, analytic exercise but to recognise that many familiar drama activities can be used to evoke responses in creative ways. Instead of just seeing pupils as theatre critics required to make analytic judgements, room can be made for more intuitive reactions. It is important of course, in avoiding mechanistic attention to form, not to make the mistake of only concentrating on content.

- Tableaux can be used to try to recreate the most significant moment from a performance or to seek to capture the central theme.

- Questioning in role (particularly of the actors after a performance) can demonstrate understanding by the questioners as much as the respondents. Enacting alternate scenes can reveal pupils' understanding of form and style as well as their grasp of content.

- 'Mantle of the expert' technique combined with play within a play can provide a framework within the drama for responding (e.g. time travellers are trying to pass themselves off as an authentic group of actors).

- Teacher in role can be seen as a way of teaching about responding because the signs have to be read appropriately.

- 'Living through' drama similarly requires the ability to read and respond to signs as the drama experience unfolds.

Responding to drama can also be helped by work which takes place in advance of a performance. The following list of suggestions has been adapted from Fleming (2001).

- Take the opening scene of the play and attempt to sketch an appropriate set – the pupils' efforts can be retained for comparison after the performance.

- Examine stage directions and decide what needs to be done at different stages in the production.

- Take specific key moments in the play and decide what symbolic action might be appropriate (e.g. does King Lear tear the map when he is dividing his kingdom?) – the moments can be selected more effectively if the teacher has seen the performance in advance.

- Try performing different short extracts using various pieces of furniture (two chairs either side of a table as opposed to a long couch).

- Decide how the ending of the play should be staged (use of curtains, lights, music, position of actors).

- Decide how a scene could be played differently in order to emphasise or minimise the humour.

- Use stylised props (e.g. a piece of card saying 'money') to see what effect this has.

- Invent an unusual performance for an extract.

Video

Differences of opinion about the appropriateness of performance need to take account of the effects of technological developments. The easy availability of portable video cameras means that drama work can be easily recorded, thereby occupying a position which is neither performance-oriented (in the sense that it is communicating there and then to an audience) nor drama for its own sake in the strictest sense. It is important to distinguish between the use of video to create a record of the drama and the making of drama using film and video techniques. In the former case the camera remains static as if from the vantage point of a member of the audience and simply records the action which unfolds before the lens. The alternative approach is to use the full facilities provided by the camera as a central constituent of the meaning of the final product (varying the camera position, using the focal length of the lens to provide close-ups, fading in and out to signify beginnings and ends of scenes, using editing facilities, changing location and so on). As one might expect, the two approaches are not discrete. Even when the camera is intended simply to provide a record of the drama, it cannot fail to frame the action in some way and direct the attention of any audience who may eventually view the filmed version. The camera lens is selective in what it records, at the very least excluding some of the extraneous background which, although it may be of little importance to the final effect, does illustrate that watching a recording of a piece of drama is different from watching the drama itself. The video camera in the drama lesson is likely to function as more than just an all seeing eye but may provide continuity of performance where there were breaks in the original action.

Pupils are surrounded by dramatic action all the time on television and on film, and it is important to recognise the difference between film (or television) drama and what might be termed 'live' performances. Nevertheless it is useful to make the distinction between 'live' and 'film' drama because the process of signification in each is different in important respects. 'Film' drama uses the potential of the camera to contribute to the meaning of the product. Soap operas, cop shows, television plays are likely for many pupils to be the major source of their tacit understanding of the dramatic process and it is important therefore for the teacher (and ultimately the pupils) to understand some of the ways in which the signifying processes of the two forms differ. Many young pupils are influenced by television and are thus frustrated by their own inability to match their own drama work to what they have seen on the screen, not simply in relation to content but also to form.

For example, a group of pupils had been asked to prepare in groups a television report based on the expedition which had been the subject of their drama for the previous three weeks. They wanted to convey the impression of using sub-titles at one point in the programme and found it technically difficult. The use of a piece of paper held by one pupil rushing across the 'screen' only produced laughter and reduced the impact of what was otherwise an effective and inventive piece of work. It is not uncommon for pupils in their dramatic play to want to 'drive' from place to place instead of using a simple dramatic convention that location can change easily without necessarily showing the physical journey. Chairs and a steering wheel are used to simulate a car and the result is often so far-fetched that it is difficult for pupils to sustain belief in the work. Simulated car crashes are not uncommon but rarely successful. Pupils who create drama about ghosts and poltergeists will often want objects to fly around the room. Imaginative ideas such as the use of flash-backs and dream sequences may be thwarted in practice because the means of representation is borrowed from film (e.g. trying to show a wavy line or out of focus effects); alternative methods such as using verbal cues would be more suitable.

The negative effect on the serious commitment to the drama produced by such 'play' activities accounts for the way the teacher's role has been emphasised in the drama in education tradition and the pupils' responsibility for devising drama given less emphasis. Recognition of the derivation of not just content but form and techniques from film drama will help both the teacher's and the pupils' own ability to create 'studio' drama. Pupils derive from television an expectation that drama should always be naturalistic; part of their dramatic education must be to extend their understanding and use of dramatic forms. For example, they need to understand characteristics of film drama as described in the following list:

- Location can be changed very easily without confusion.

- The camera can guide the eye of the spectator. Attention can be focused on precise detail – e.g. bullets were actually removed from a gun, a document is stolen, an important event happens in a crowded place such as a disco.

- Flash-backs and dream sequences can be signalled through camera techniques.

- Close-up on people's faces can be used to convey emotional intensity.

- Slow motion and (less frequently) speeded up film may be used to create special effects. (The use of slow motion can be used in drama but often it is hard for pupils to believe in what they are doing.)

- There is no possibility of interaction between actors and film audience.

- Editing provides an extra level of control of meaning for the film maker.

- A whole range of special effects may be employed (twins as doubles, split frames, the ability for items to appear and disappear, objects moving of their own accord, appearing many times their actual size).

Whether drama is being used across the curriculum or taught as a separate subject, there are advantages in using video both as a straightforward record of work undertaken and, more elaborately, to create film. A recording of the drama work can provide motivation and a focus for future reflection and analysis. It can also be very valuable for one class or group to see the work of another as a stimulus for their own efforts; it was suggested in an earlier chapter that the over-emphasis on creativity as originality has tended to inhibit the use of examples in this way.

Using video to create a simple film needs more specific attention to technicalities. It goes without saying that if media studies is taught in the school then some liaison is required; that is a matter for the school curriculum policy which was discussed in Chapter 2. Availability of equipment is clearly a factor, but the camera can be integrated into the drama in some imaginative ways. For example, it is possible to have the camera take the place of one of the characters so that the audience watching the video see all the action through that character's eyes (Cutler-Gray and Taylor 1991).

Being alert to the more obvious mistakes which pupils (and teachers) are likely to make when new to filming can save much wasted effort. These are:

- using the zoom facility too rapidly and too frequently;

- panning the camera (i.e. moving it across a scene) far too quickly;

- failing to recognise that built in microphones pick up the speech of the camera operator more readily than they do the actors;

- failing to keep the camera steady;

- cutting off the ends and beginnings of scenes;

- filming against the light so that faces are in darkness.

Use of video needs to be seen in the wider context of ICT. Theatre technology has developed considerably in recent years and will form part of the drama curriculum for older pupils. Multi-media can be used creatively to enhance performance and the Internet is being increasingly used as a research tool. The further reading section of this chapter provides details of more extended treatment of these issues.

Drama and the school community

This concluding section will begin with an example of a drama project which took place at the Sacred Heart Primary School, Barnet, which culminated in a performance of *Evacuees*, a play based on the evacuation of children from London before the war in the late 1930s. On the evening of the performance the audience entered the school lobby to be met by a large collage on the wall with accompanying class work based on the blitz, and to hear the strains of Vera Lynn and other war-time songs coming from the school hall. Every visitor received a programme and although the content of each was the same the covers were different, for they had been designed by the large numbers of pupils who had taken part in the production. When the audience assembled in the hall the Head teacher, Mrs Ruane, made a brief introductory speech. She welcomed the visitors and said how much the school would miss the Year 6 pupils who were about to perform; they had contributed so much to the school and had been generous towards each other and mutually supportive.

Even before the start of the play, the framing devices were contributing to its overall meaning. This was more than just a school production; it was the very last week for these pupils in the school and the event acted as a community celebration and a marking of a significant ending and a new beginning for them. The choice of play was therefore particularly poignant dealing as it does with farewells and separation from family. The fact that the audience consisted largely of parents or older relatives who experienced evacuation from London during the war also contributed to the strength of response to its subject matter. The wall displays revealed that the play had been integrated with the work of the normal curriculum and had provided a focus for much classroom activity in preceding weeks. The programmes which celebrated the efforts of so many of the pupils indicated that the ethos of the production had not been to isolate and celebrate stars, the most talented artists and best actors, but had sought to recognise and value the contributions of all participants. The introductory music and the simple stage design and lighting set the scene for a high quality production.

In fact the quality of the work surprised many members of the audience who came with memories of their own school plays, of lines recited parrot fashion and embarrassed silences and stage mishaps. It would be tempting to assume that the pupils had been rehearsing the play for an inordinate amount of time, such was the high standard of their performance, but in fact the opposite was the case; the rehearsal work was intensive but lasted only three weeks.

Work on the play began in drama lessons, using what has traditionally been viewed as drama in education techniques including various forms of improvisation. As one of the pupils commented, 'We put a lot of things in that weren't in the script, which made it more interesting.' Understanding of content was therefore of primary concern and this was enhanced by the considerable amount of work undertaken on the topic in the school curriculum. A visit to the Imperial War Museum (which, from the interviews conducted with the pupils, had clearly made a significant impression) was accompanied by work on primary and secondary sources such as film footage, radio broadcasts, photographs and artefacts. Full advantage was taken of the opportunity to integrate history (time line, sequencing events, considering the outbreak of war, education, the home front), geography (exploring a map of Europe in the context of the war), and language work (letters home, the subtle changes in the language of the time, newspaper articles and the exploration of bias and opinion). Art work contributed to the programme and ticket design, the blitz collage and pastel silhouettes; music had a very definite contribution in considering the popular styles of the period and rehearsing the relevant songs.

Understanding of content therefore was a major consideration but that was not the only important factor. Prior to the production, drama work focused specifically on stage techniques and these were approached with a sense of real purpose.

What are the general principles which can be evolved from this example?

Choice of play

The teachers responsible for this project took care to ensure that the choice of work was suitable for the pupils. In this case the inclusion of songs and the nature of the subject matter was chosen with those pupils in mind to reflect their abilities and interests. Cultural considerations are also important and it is unwise to assume that a work which has been successful in one context will be appropriate every-where. Performance work can be evolved from classroom improvisation or, as in this case, the script can be enhanced and given more ownership to the pupils by incorporating their contributions.

Aims

The project illustrates that a number of different aims can be fulfilled in harmony in work of this kind. Pupils were clearly gaining an understanding of drama as a discipline and art form as well as developing their understanding of the subject matter. The teachers concerned, however, were also eager to stress the personal and social development which was a tacit aspect of the process. For the project to succeed it demanded a considerable degree of mutual respect, cooperation and support from the pupils involved.

Curriculum integration

It is not only improvised classroom drama which can contribute to the curriculum. In this example the National Curriculum was comfortably integrated as part of the background work on the project. Improvised work was used in drama to enhance understanding and to contribute to the development of the theme prior to the specific focus on the staging of the play.

Lighting and costume

Part of the value of the project was that pupils were learning about stagecraft but such items as lighting and costume were subordinate to the meaning of the play and did not dominate as simple ends in themselves. The pupils who played the part of evacuees in the production were given the task of researching and equipping themselves with their own costumes; they made gas mask boxes in technology. Lighting was simple but effective, altering to signify time and location, with the occasional use of spotlights to highlight particular characters.

Time-scale

It is sometimes argued that school productions take up too much time. In this case, with a year group who had experience of drama as part of their normal curriculum and because earlier class work had been devoted to the theme, the rehearsal time lasted an intensive three weeks. Other projects may need more time but if the work provides a focus for other National Curriculum activities then this factor is less of an issue. Clearly for a project to be successful in a short time-scale the pupils need to be highly motivated and aware that the work requires considerable dedication.

Further reading

Frameworks and lists of questions to help pupils respond to plays can be found in a chapter by Urian in Hornbrook, D. (ed.) (1998b) *On the Subject of Drama* and Neelands, J. and Dobson, W. (2000) *Drama and Theatre Studies at AS/A Level*. For an approach to studying plays see Wallis, M. and Shepherd, S. (1998) *Studying Plays*. Bennett, S. (1990) *Theatre Audiences* provides an examination of the role of the spectator with a particular focus on non-traditional theatres. Harrop, J. (1992) *Acting* provides a theoretical overview of this subject. See also Fortier, M. (1997) *Theory/Theatre: An Introduction* on literacy theory and performance. For accounts which yield many insights into the nature and evolution of performance see Casdagli, P. and Gobey, F. with Griffin, C. (1992) *Grief* and (1990) *Only Playing*; Dodgson, E. (1984) *Motherland*. Links to drama websites can be found through *www.nationaldrama.co.uk*

CHAPTER

9

Progression and assessment

Progress in drama

DESCRIBING PROGRESSION IN DRAMA is not straightforward yet it is important because without a coherent account of how pupils make progress in the subject it is very difficult to decide how drama should be assessed. Nor is it possible to plan in a coherent and balanced way without some sense of how work can be made increasingly challenging. In order to understand why progression has caused such difficulties for writers on drama it is useful to distinguish between 'descriptive' accounts (the way in which drama is thought to develop naturally) and 'prescriptive' accounts (the way in which drama should develop as a result of being specifically taught). These distinctions will become clearer in the light of an exploration of the general problems involved in describing progression.

Attempts to apply the notion of progression to human learning, particularly in the arts, can be extremely bewildering. We know that human beings develop in various ways (cognitively, emotionally, physically, aesthetically and so on) but attempts to describe progression in learning in successive stages can easily lead to distorted and over-simplified accounts. It is difficult enough to give a coherent account of human development; it is even more of a challenge to describe in systematic fashion the learning which is to come about by virtue of being taught. As a teacher, unless one subscribes to extremely rigid and narrow orthodoxies, it is easy to be attracted simultaneously to two competing positions. An intuitive grasp of the unfathomable richness and complexity of human learning (which while deeply felt may have limited functional value in teaching because of its vagueness) may be contrasted with the quasi-scientific, objective but ultimately reductive attempts to analyse that diversity into specific stages. Logic and rationality point to the need for specific objectives identified in progressive stages. How else can teachers know what they are trying to achieve and how they are going to help their pupils to make progress? Moreover, how else are they going to inform the outside world of pupils' achievements?

Such arguments are compelling but attempts to develop attainment targets and levels are vulnerable to criticism because they often constitute only a partial reflection of the subject they are trying to describe. On the other hand, accounts of progression which try to do justice to the complexities involved can easily become unworkable. Statements which seek to describe progress in a subject are likely to involve some degree of reduction and simplification; the appropriate question therefore seems to be not so much whether such endeavours are worthwhile but whether in the process they distort the essential nature of the subject.

The idea of trying to evolve a developmental perspective for drama is by no means new. Slade's framework was derived from years of observation of children at play. In his work we find the idea that certain manifestations of drama such as performance on stage and work on the scripted play are appropriate only at particular ages. Slade was drawing on experience in the 1940s and it is likely, with the wider exposure to television which children receive today, that their sense of dramatic form will develop earlier; cultural experience is a significant determining factor rather than just their natural aptitude for play. Child drama was something Slade observed rather than created and he was at pains to argue that the schooling process should mesh with the way pupils develop naturally. Courtney (1968) much later identified dramatic stages: the identification stage, the impersonation stage (10 months to 7 years), the group drama stage (7–12), the role stage (12–18). While one might want to question the details of these schemes, the broad reminder that it may be unproductive to introduce particular modes of working in drama too soon has to be taken seriously and is still relevant.

Two important characteristics of these approaches to the notion of progression distinguish them from contemporary accounts. In keeping with the educational context of the time, drama is seen here primarily as a creative, expressive subject rather than one which includes the notion of responding to drama, even though much of Slade's professional life was devoted to children's theatre. The implicit assumption which is now no longer tenable, that the reading and watching of plays is not itself an example of creativity, was an inevitable aspect of the prevailing literary and educational assumptions. Secondly the attempt here is to *describe* Piagetian-type stages of dramatic development rather than to *prescribe* the progress it was thought pupils ought to make as a result of being taught. Labelling accounts of progression as 'prescriptive' is not meant to imply any negative judgement but is simply intended to contrast with descriptive accounts. The two of course are interrelated in that prescriptive accounts need to be based on what is appropriate for particular age groups.

The prevailing climate of a liberal approach to education started after the turn of the twentieth century but gathered pace in the 1950s and 1960s, placing emphasis on the natural growth and development of the child. It was not until the late

1960s, under the guise of 'neutral' analytic philosophy, that writers like Peters launched an attack on the excesses which equated natural development with education. Much of the philosophical writing of Hirst and Peters aimed to demonstrate that teaching and learning needed to be viewed as deliberate intentional activities to distinguish them from concepts of growth and development.

One characteristic of Slade's account of progression in drama is that it was focused on dramatic modes rather than the learning or development which comes about as a result of participation in drama. The ascendancy of drama in education methodology with its emphasis on improvisation, while not neglecting dramatic form in the process of dramatic engagement, placed emphasis on the content of the lesson as the objective of the learning. In Bolton's writing the emphasis changed from describing the learning in propositional terms to a more general concept of mental development which came about as a result of the drama (Bolton 1979, 1984). It was many people's experience of drama that it challenged conventional notions of what pupils were capable of addressing and understanding in educational contexts; descriptions of lessons by Bolton and Heathcote are all marked by the sense that pupils could tackle material which in other contexts would be deemed to be beyond them. By providing contexts of feeling and meaning, pupils of all ages seemed to be able to engage deeply with moral, anthropological and philosophical questions. While drama seemed to challenge accepted popular notions of progression in teaching it was little wonder that there was minimal focus on progression within drama as a subject itself.

Influenced by National Curriculum frameworks in other subjects, writers in the 1990s started to produce more prescriptive accounts of progression using attainment targets and levels of attainment (Hornbrook 1991; Neelands 1998; Kempe and Ashwell 2000; Arts Council 2003). Three attainment targets are usually identified (creating/making; performing; responding) and levels of attainment for each one. Such schemes are useful for departments to adapt for their own use but they need to be seen as broad guidelines rather than precise structures to be used mechanistically. An understanding of some of the reasons why describing progression in drama is particularly challenging will be helpful in making sensible, flexible use of the available frameworks.

Learning does not progress in a neat linear sequence

One of the difficulties faced by teachers of all subjects who have tried to come to terms with a curriculum model which describes progression in successive stages is that learning does not proceed in a simple, straight, linear fashion. Pupils will often make progress in one aspect of a subject while seeming to regress in another. In English the ability to punctuate simple sentences can seem to be temporarily lost when more complex constructions are attempted. Thoughtless attempts to marshal pupils through predetermined stages may deny them essential prerequisites for learning: the freedom to take risks, make mistakes and experiment. In the context of drama too much belief in the efficacy of sequencing the learning has participants engaged in tedious, lengthy exercises (e.g. practising the five senses) before they are considered ready for more creative work; 'The Doctor's Visit' tape described in Chapter 5 and transcribed in Appendix A, however, illustrates that a four-year-old is capable of highly sophisticated play-making. This observation does not render the whole business of describing progression redundant but highlights the need for sensitive interpretation and application. Any attempt to isolate ability in drama from learning through drama is likely to result in pupils reaching a low ceiling of achievement because of the failure to engage with content. Imagine trying to teach the four-year-old in 'The Doctor's Visit' how to 'adopt and sustain a role in a drama' without a meaningful focus on content.

Contextual considerations affect performance

Another related difficulty is the recognition that ability in a particular sphere seems to change with context and the degree of motivation and engagement felt by the participants. It has long been recognised that the use of drama within a subject can provide considerable motivation to learning but it is less frequently acknowledged that pupils' motivation and disposition towards drama (and therefore their performance and 'ability') varies with the context. It is difficult to abstract a concept such as 'ability to do drama' from the context in which the particular aptitude is embedded. Teachers of English will readily recognise the difficulties in making judgements about oral performance for the same reason; in the novel *Kes* Billy Casper's oral performance was a function of his passion for his subject.

Role of the teacher

It has been part of the tradition of drama in education to place more emphasis on the role of the teacher in creating successful drama than on the pupils' capacity to do so. This point was made in Chapter 1 and it can partly be explained by the reaction against the minimal role given to the teacher in the more extreme child-centred approaches. It was generally accepted by exponents of drama in education that an effective teacher would be able to create drama which was both educationally and aesthetically worthwhile with any class or group irrespective of their previous experience. In fact it was often assumed that less experienced pupils would be easier to work with because they would be unsullied by superficial approaches. Such attitudes arose in a context in which there was a reaction both to the rather formless dramatic play to be found in an approach which simply asked pupils to 'get into groups and do a play' and to the overuse of sensory exercises and activities in which the teacher merely directed the action: 'Time to get up . . . stretch . . . have a good wash . . .'

There are then a considerable number of difficulties involved in describing progression in drama but they are not dissimilar to those faced by English teachers who know that making progress in 'writing' does not just mean grasping what have been termed 'secretarial' skills. It is clear from the above discussion that to attempt to isolate some notion of ability in drama from any focus on subject matter is likely to result in a reductive and simplistic account of the subject.

Although the nature of the role of the teacher has been a crucial consideration in describing developments in drama teaching, it needs also to inform discussions about progression in drama. As pupils gain experience in the subject, they should be able to use dramatic forms to create meaning independently of the teacher. However, if they are left to their own devices in the early stages there is a great danger that they will never experience anything except 'ham acting' or the rough and tumble of dramatic playing.

The following considerations then need to inform progression in drama.

- When drama is taught as a separate subject, progression needs to be described in terms of its own subject-specific criteria.

- It is the *pupils'* progress in drama which needs to be described.

- As pupils progress through junior and secondary school they need to have some awareness of the objectives of the work and the criteria for assessment.

- Statements of criteria require exemplification in order to be easily communicable.

- Frameworks should be seen as broad indicators of how pupils make progress and not definitive accounts of the subject.

Variety in drama

It is easy to see the concept of 'variety' as having rather more superficial connotations than that of 'progression'. Variety is helpful to alleviate boredom, to provide a fresh impetus to a familiar theme. However, the notion of variety also has deeper educational significance in that varying pupils' experience in drama is important in order to give breadth of curriculum experience. Also, providing alternative methodologies or using different dramatic conventions with respect to a particular issue can deepen understanding. The concepts of 'progression' and 'variety' are related in that when devising programmes of study the opportunity for pupils to progress is in part provided by engaging them in different themes using a variety of techniques, approaches and starting points.

The principles identified above in relation to describing progression should inform the planning of schemes of work as discussed in Chapter 3. The idea that students need to practise basic skills in drama before they can attempt work with significant content can have dangerous consequences. The fact that a group who are totally new to drama can be led to produce drama work of extraordinary power has always presented something of an enigma when trying to describe progression, but not if it is recognised that schemes of work should be constructed in ways which gradually hand over more responsibility to the participants for constructing the drama.

It is very easy for one approach to drama to become dominant. The following section then is intended to provide a reminder of the range of possible approaches which can be adapted to different topics and for different ages. Most of them are relevant both in the teaching of drama and in the use of drama across the curriculum.

Variety can be provided by changing the orientation (making, performing, responding), mode (script, planned and unplanned improvisation), organisation (pairs, small group, whole group) and conventions used in the drama. It is also a good idea to vary the starting point by using artefacts, documents, literary sources and games. Objects (a box, an old book, a photograph frame, a bunch of keys) can be used in order to seek ideas from the pupils or to engage the class in the lesson which has been planned by the teacher in advance. The advantage of this as a starting point is that the object provides a concrete focus for the drama and is likely to accrue greater symbolic force as the work progresses: it needs to function as more than just a prop. For example, the drama might explore the way a particular possession (such as a writing desk or frame) featured in different generations in a family. An old book might be used to create a drama about the past: 'What secret was discovered in this book which changed the lives of the people who owned it?' Roman artefacts would provide a useful focus for combining history and drama whereby the class in role as actors are invited to help the historians recreate scenes depicting how those objects might have been used.

Newspaper headlines and articles are interesting starting points for drama because they rarely present more than an outline of the particular story and often only present one opinion. The drama can seek to examine the real human story behind the headline or to present two versions of the same account. An article about UFOs was used as a starting point to explore the question 'What would make someone invent a story of this kind?' (see p. 132). The use of legend and myth can help to move the drama beyond the social realism which pupils will often revert to if left to their own choices. Alternatively, using poems to initiate the drama can bring a fresh perspective to familiar themes as described in Chapter 7.

Drama examples

This section gives a brief description of some projects which newcomers to drama have found useful. They should be read in the context of the various comments made in the Introduction about the difficulties involved in translating ideas on paper into practical activities in the classroom. There are a large number of variables which influence the way any class reacts to a particular lesson or activity. However, given that much of this book has been concerned with highlighting the sorts of difficulties and problems which can arise in drama lessons, it is hoped that some of these structures will provide helpful starting points for teachers wishing to devise their own activities. In each case a very bald summary of the sequence of the project as it was taught is given, followed by contextual considerations, discussion of drama-specific objectives and, where relevant, ideas for extending the project.

Dinosaurs (Key Stage 2)

1 Pupils play the Keys of the Kingdom game (see Chapter 4).

2 They are invited to imagine that a large animal, perhaps a dinosaur, is sleeping where the keeper was placed. A volunteer creeps forward to retrieve the keys without waking the animal. Several others take turns to do so in silence while the teacher contributes to the tension by insisting in a whisper that the others do not make a sound.

3 Dinosaurs and man never lived at the same time on earth. However, what reasons might the local people have for being suspicious (but not certain) that there are dinosaurs in the area?

4 The class report their suspicions to the teacher in role as an official who is sceptical of their claims but asks for more evidence.

5 The class go off in pairs to collect evidence – footprints, dimensions, drawings, etc.

6 This time the sceptical official is a little more convinced and accompanies the class to inspect some of their findings.

7 The class make a list of the facts they feel they need to find out now about dinosaurs.

Ambiguity was a central element of this project and provided the necessary dramatic tension: dinosaurs never actually featured in the play, any evidence which was produced to verify their existence was not conclusive proof. In this way the pupils' belief in the drama was built by having an adult who was very sceptical about their find: they could only convince him by taking the situation seriously themselves. The lesson aimed to create a context and a motivation for research on dinosaurs, to teach about skills of deduction and to involve the pupils in contexts which required them to use language to give explanations and justify reasoning. They were also learning how to work to sustain the drama by not introducing extraneous factors which would deny the illusion: in other words it was essential that no pupil introduced wild evidence of dinosaurs rampaging around the countryside or eating herds of cows. This needs to be addressed explicitly by the teacher as an important drama-specific objective and moves the work along the continuum from 'playing' towards the art form. If the appropriate attitude and mood are fostered the references to dinosaurs will remain oblique. One class who enacted this drama went with the 'official' to investigate a cave. The group assembled and with echoes of the Keys of the Kingdom game one pupil slowly entered and very carefully brought out an imaginary egg.

The start of this lesson is an example of building the drama from the 'outside in': in other words concentrating on getting the surface action right before turning to ideas and content. The distinction between 'internal' and 'external' action is discussed in more detail in Chapter 10. It is important for the subsequent development of the lesson that the pupils act out the initial mime in a way which creates the appropriate mood of serious commitment. Pupils tend to be familiar with the quasi-scientific fantasy that dinosaurs might genetically be recreated in a modern era and this feeds into the drama. That does not mean that they are not able to speculate on possible explanations for the 'evidence': another large animal, film publicity, a hoax. Their drawings of such items as footprints, skin left on trees, undergrowth having been trampled, animal carcasses, do not have to be scientifically accurate for the drama to proceed but create a motivation for research afterwards. Similarly the work can be extended to consider mathematical concepts of dimensions (how large would a footprint be?), scale (what size would the clay replica have to be?), weight (how deep would the footprint be in soft ground?).

The Mysterious Mansion (Key Stage 2)

1 The pupils are shown two large keys which will be used for the basis of their drama work.

2 One key has magic powers and can temporarily turn people to stone. The class practise freezing and unfreezing at a wave of the keys in the form of a game or exercise.

3 The other key opens the door to a large mansion which is situated on the outskirts of the village in which the pupils live.

4 Who lives in the mansion and why is it that the pupils would like to get inside? Here the teacher is giving the pupils an initiative within the drama but is aware that whatever their answer, it is possible to proceed with the lesson structure as planned.

5 Pupils visit the mansion and try to talk their way in past the servant who opens the door.

6 Eventually the pupils persuade the servant to let them in but the other key is used to control their movements, turning them into stone if necessary.

7 The pupils decide how the story will develop, which can be narrated by the teacher with some scenes enacted.

This project was originally negotiated with the class by using the keys as a starting point. It has been redescribed here, however, to provide a more secure and tight framework. Given the magical element introduced by the teacher at the start of the first lesson the pupils' responses to the question 'who lives in the mansion?' are fairly predictable; nevertheless it is important that they are given some control over the direction of the narrative particularly if they are to decide later how it will develop. The scene in which the pupils try to persuade the servant to let them in can be enacted in different ways: either the class can present themselves as a whole group, or two or three individuals at a time can try with others watching. The teacher uses the role to challenge the pupils and elevate their language. Here the drama-specific objective centres on responding to the signs represented through the role and exercising restraint in order to build tension. Here the other key can be useful because the pupils are more likely to want to turn this into a physical rather than linguistic exercise ('let's knock him on the head', 'climb in a window'). Of course there is no reason why the drama should not develop in its own way if the pupils are committed and the teacher feels confident in allowing it to do so. Here one pupil's description of his encounter with the owner of the castle is presented in a rather breathless style as he describes the way in which the man's story was disproved. He also conveys what turned out to be the central point of the drama, which was that the owner was really a rather lonely person.

'We came back to the castle again. When we got there the owner of the castle asked us what we were doing outside his castle and what we wanted. After much persuading he let us come into his castle. Before we entered we had to take off our shoes so that there wouldn't be any muddy footprints all over the castle. When we were inside we had a look around the place which was as clean as new fallen snow which meant he wasn't the only person who lived in the castle because he said that his servant only got the firewood and lit the fire. So we asked more questions. He was getting worried so he turned us all into stone statues then he released us. This proved that he was a liar because the castle was clean and his servant only got the firewood and lit the fire and the master of the castle wouldn't clean his castle unless the keys or one of them could do it for him which they might seeing as they turned us to stone statues which is another reason why I think he was a liar because he said that the keys were just ordinary keys. Then he let us into his big secret. He said he just wanted some friends. I said that we would be his friends if he promised not to turn us into stone. Then I told him that you don't make friends by putting people in dungeons . . .'

UFOs (Key Stage 3)

1 A newspaper headline article is shown to the class – e.g. 'My encounter with an alien'. This can be simply written on the board if an article is not available. The class are asked how they react to the headline and whether they believe in such claims. The question is posed: 'What would make someone invent a story of this kind?'

2 They question teacher in role as someone who claims to have seen a UFO to see if the story is true. They are then placed in role as a government-sponsored body which has been set up to investigate reported sightings. They establish their identity at a meeting in which they discuss such matters as the spending of the budget (do they need a new telescope or computer?), a recent case which turned out to be a hoax, and the financial difficulties and possible job losses they might have to face.

3 In groups the pupils as investigators conduct their official interviews of those who claimed to have spotted a UFO. There is a dual tension; the situation has been set up on the basis that they might be telling lies but the progress of the drama relies on establishing the truth of at least one of the sightings. The teacher in role as boss insists that money must not be wasted if the group expects to continue to receive funding.

4 Class report back to their superior on what they have discovered. They decide which story is worth investigating further and proceed to the site to record more interviews, measurements, drawings, etc.

5 It is possible now to extend the project by allowing groups to devise and present to the rest of the class the outcome of their investigation.

This lesson was first taught with the luxury of having drama students in role as people with stories to tell about their 'sightings'. Because they were strangers to the pupils the reality of the situation fed into the fiction; which of these people whom we have never met before is telling lies? Pupils can be used in this role but in that case it is helpful to deliver actual letters with reported sightings to the investigation team for them to sift through first. They can then decide which letter they will choose for further investigation. This project aims to build belief in the content slowly by basing the drama on the assumption that most UFO sightings are false trails, which contributes to the building of dramatic tension.

Fire of London (Key Stage 3)

1 The class are introduced to the topic by being asked what they know about it. After pooling their knowledge, they are told that a Committee of Enquiry was set up after the fire to establish the cause and whether so much damage could have been avoided once it had started.

2   Creation of tableaux entitled 'Fire of London'. These are read with the question in mind – how do we tell this scene happened a long time ago? The class are then asked to create the sounds of voices which might have accompanied the scenes (the shouts of panic are more effective if played over an audio-recording of fire).

3   Class are given roles (one role to a group) along with source material – e.g. letter from Lady Hobart writing from her home in Chancery Lane on 4 September 1666, extract from the diary of Pepys, eye-witness account of the Mayor's actions, testimony of Thomas Farynor the baker, experts who will report on the timber construction of the houses. Each group is asked to prepare a television 'drama documentary' (including interviews and dramatised scenes) presenting each individual's evidence. At the centre of the investigation will be one central character created in some depth.

4   The scenes are viewed, revised and woven together to present an investigative account of the Fire of London.

5   Accounts of the Committee of Enquiry held at the time are distributed and discussed.

6   As a follow up the class might consider the difficulties involved in dealing with a subject like 'fire' in live drama as opposed to in film.

Groups are likely to need help in order to see ways of expanding and interpreting the material. It is a good idea for the teacher to have some suggestions to feed in to each group so that they can make progress. There is nothing worse than a group saying to a teacher in drama 'We can't think of anything to do' and the teacher suddenly saying to himself 'Neither can I'. Although the drama is factually based, at its centre is an emphasis on creating character through developing contextual details and background information, explained in brief clues contained in the papers (e.g. the mayor clearly drank a great deal).

This does happen and can be avoided if one possible outcome for each group's task is thought through before the lesson. In this lesson the drama helped to create a context for the acquisition of knowledge about the Fire of London as well as exploring the ways in which deductions are made from source material. One of the central themes turned out to be the way the fire affected the rich and poor.

The 'Ad Family' (Key Stage 3)

1   The class are shown a very stylised cartoon drawing of an idealised family from the world of advertising or an advert depicting such a perfect family. They list typical attributes: they never argue, mother never gets harassed, father is always patient, brother and sister are always cooperative, house is always perfectly tidy.

2   Groups are asked to act out a simple breakfast time by showing the family as they appear in idealised form in the advert. Their representations can be stylised and exaggerated.

3   One group is chosen or volunteers to be the 'ad family', each of whom will now form a new group in order to depict a scene which shows the reality of their lives as opposed to the false version they present to one another. These scenes might involve the adults at work, the children at play with friends or at school.

4   The scenes are revised and polished, and a sequence worked out.

5   The results are video-recorded.

The contrast between appearance and reality is a useful focus for dramatic exploration (and is a central feature of much literature). This drama is a variation on a more familiar theme that the reality of family life is very different from the truth presented to the outside world (which could also be explored in similar fashion). The project is suitable for an experienced class in drama but even so it is not intended that all groups perform their version of the 'ad family' at stage two. In most classes there are individuals who have more of a propensity for the type of satirical, stylised depiction which this scene requires. However, the key dramatic objective relates to experimenting with different styles. Other pupils in the class are likely to find more comfortable roles in the other scenes, hence the purpose of choosing or asking for a volunteer group. In this project the 'ad family' used simple masks when they were presenting their false selves which they subsequently discarded in the 'reality' scenes. The work could be extended into more elaborate use of masks.

Homeless (Key Stage 4)

1   A picture of a homeless person is used to introduce the topic.

2   Sitting separately facing the picture, the class one by one articulate the thoughts and memories of the person as the end of his/her life draws near. These may be in the form of direct speech (memories of a teacher's or parent's voice), or the person's own thoughts set in the past or present ('I can't afford to lose this job, I just can't', 'If they don't stop I'm going to leave home').

3   The teacher feeds back to the class the comments made and starts to create a picture of the person's life story.

4   One member of the class is chosen to play the part of the homeless person and the rest in groups are given the task of preparing a piece of drama which deals with an aspect of that person's life. The homeless person will circulate around the groups. One item (an object, song or verse of a poem) will reappear in each scene.

5   The pupils perform their rough version of each scenario establishing the context within the drama through exposition rather than using narrative. They modify each extract to create consistency. Teacher and pupils discuss the ways in which each group's work might be improved and the ways in which lighting, music and props might be used for the final version.

6   The work as a whole is performed in the form of a 'flash-back' of the person's life.

The theme of homelessness was chosen by the teacher rather than negotiated and it was therefore felt necessary to introduce the topic to the pupils by means of a concrete starting point. A photograph of a man obviously worn and living rough was covered with paper, leaving the eyes and a small portion of the face showing. This aroused the curiosity of the class who were invited to speculate about the meaning of what the eyes conveyed about the content of what was concealed. Only a brief amount of time was spent on this activity because, unlike many of the questions posed in a drama lesson, there was a right answer – there is little point in encouraging pupils to become involved in their own interpretation if these were not going to be considered as possible subject matter for the drama. The introductory activity is more a way of arousing interest before the unveiling of the rest of the photograph. The revelation of the photograph has parallels with 'curtain up' in a stage performance and the teacher was able to make parallels with the expectations caused by the set of a stage play.

After establishing that this was in fact a picture of a homeless person, pupils offered their accounts of who he might be and the sort of life he might lead. A slide of the photograph projected onto a wall provided the focus for articulating voices from the character's past. This was a key moment of the lesson and its success gave considerable momentum to the work which followed. It is important that it is set up carefully. The class are to speak those thoughts aloud as they think it appropriate; if they wish they may stay silent; none must speak except to contribute to the thoughts of the character; if two people start to speak at once this need not be a problem if one or other is simply allowed to go first. It is worth telling the class that the exercise may seem a little strange at first but if done properly it will be very effective. They should not worry too much if the thoughts do not seem to have a consistency. Examples might be: 'This is the third week in a row you haven't paid the rent. . . . You can't sleep here sir. . . . I'm not being your friend. . . .'

The success of the above exercise largely depends on the confidence with which it is approached by the teacher. It is worth considering what contingency plans might be required in this situation. It is possible that the pupils will be silent and will have nothing to offer either because they are embarrassed or simply because they genuinely cannot think of anything to say. In this case the exercise can be repeated with less spontaneity. The class divide into pairs and are invited to prepare together a brief statement. The pairs are then numbered and the thoughts articulated in sequence. This approach can be used if the more spontaneous version is causing some pupils to giggle. In the case of contributions which serve to destroy the serious commitment to the work then this problem will not be solved by subtle manoeuvres within the drama. It is a disciplinary matter which requires that the teacher makes it clear that such contributions are unhelpful and inhibiting the progress of the work. The pupils were asked to contribute positively or simply to listen and it is fair to expect them to cooperate to that extent. Notice this is a very different situation from one in which pupils react inappropriately in drama because they are embarrassed about what they have been asked to do.

I have dwelt some time on this preliminary exercise because its success makes an important contribution to the quality of the rest of the project. With the right motivation and emotional engagement which a successful creation of the character's thoughts can instil, the small-group scenes based on aspects of the homeless person's life have more depth. Also, the success of the first exercise may encourage groups to experiment with non-naturalistic forms. The teacher needs to listen carefully to the pupils' contributions in order to feed them back in summary form. For example, 'This person once had a very happy and supportive home life but seems to have left home because of an argument . . . he does not appear to have got on well in school. . . .' The identification of an object (music box, photograph, toy), verse or song which will appear in the first scene and which will later reappear in the drama helps to give pupils an insight into symbolism in a very straightforward way.

The objectives here are clearly related to the acquisition of knowledge of the way symbolism operates in drama but the pupils are also exploring notions of free will and determinism in relation to human experience: could this person's life have turned out other than it did?

The Crucible (Key Stage 4)

1 Pupils create family groups, each with a teenage daughter.

2 While the teenage daughters form a group of their own, the families prepare a scene which shows that some of them have suspicions that the teenager is dabbling in black magic. Other family members think this is nonsense.

3 The girls meanwhile decide in secret why it was that they as a group were meeting in the local woods at midnight; they might have an explanation which has nothing to do with witchcraft but whatever it is they do not want their parents to know.

4 The families have found out that the girls have been seen in the woods and confront them with the information.

5 The families meet with teacher in role as chair; panic and scapegoating start to take hold.

6 The girls create a tableau which depicts the real reason for being in the woods.

7 Copies of The Crucible are distributed and the class read Act One. In groups they now create a tableau of where actors might be on stage as the first act is completed.

8 The different groups work on staging a scene from the Crucible.

This drama explores the concept of 'moral panic' but also provides an introduction to further work on *The Crucible*. The teacher here gives quite strong direction to each scene but the lack of knowledge of the genuine explanation for the girls' actions provides impetus to the work. It is important that there is ambiguity about the girls' actions and therefore about the cause of the families' worry; this also helps give impetus to the presentation of that initial scene where the family members disagree. It is possible to let the drama take its own course at the point when the meeting takes place but this requires skilful and subtle direction from the teacher if the drama is not to become static. In the course of the work pupils can develop quite rounded characterisations and develop relationships within and between families.

Table 9.1 highlights the way in which the demands in terms of the drama focus increases progressively through the topics. The list in the right-hand column does not represent all of the drama focuses in each project but highlights those which underline the progression. This in itself shows the complexity of the concept because many lessons begin with games and warm-up exercises no matter how sophisticated the participants.

TABLE 9.1 Example of progression in drama

Theme	Drama focus
Dinosaurs	Ability to adopt simple roles. Moving from 'playing' to 'dramatic art' by accepting constraints of delaying the climax.
The Mysterious Mansion	Reading and responding to the signs of teacher in role. Creating short enacted scenes guided by teacher narration.
UFOs	Creating short enacted scenes independently of teacher narration. Building dramatic tension by withholding information.
Fire of London	Distinguishing between character and role. Creating character by working on background detail.
The 'Ad' Family	Devising stylised, non-naturalistic drama. Using masks to enhance the impact of the drama.
Homelessness	Understanding and creating different drama structures. Understanding the importance of exposition and using the concept in creating drama. Devising complex scenes using different time frames.
The Crucible	Turning a play script into dramatic performance. Devising small-group drama independently.

The starting points for these lessons varied from a simple physical game (the dinosaur lesson) to an invitation to talk about the theme (the Fire of London): 'internal' and 'external' dimensions in drama, a distinction which has been touched on earlier in this book, will be the subject of more detailed discussion in the final chapter.

Assessing drama

To make sense of progression and assessment in drama (and indeed in all subjects) it is necessary to abandon notions of exactitude and precision and think more in terms of broad indicators and approximations. Tolerance of 'rough edges' is easier when using progression frameworks to plan schemes of work but feels less appropriate in the case of assessment because making judgements about pupils' attainment should not be taken lightly. However, it is important to recognise that only trivial forms of assessment can claim strict objectivity and there will always be an element of uncertainty in the whole process.

Assessment criteria are often written with a tacit belief that language is transparent, with an assumption that if the criteria are specific and detailed enough, there will be no room for disagreement or misinterpretation. Thus assessment schemes tend to become more and more detailed in an attempt to dispel ambiguity. But this is to direct energy in the wrong area. It is not in the refining of language that assessment schemes become more consistent but in the exemplification of what is meant by a particular statement. Consider the following statements drawn from different assessment schemes and try to envisage what they mean: 'show awareness of self on drama', 'maintain narrative consistency within the drama', 'responding to and using elements of the form'. In order to be able to come to an agreement that a pupil is meeting any of these criteria to an appropriate level it would be far more helpful to have concrete examples of what is meant rather than further refinement of the statements.

Another reason why assessment schemes tend to become increasingly complex is in the quest for validity. 'Validity' is the term used to describe whether a form of assessment actually does measure what it claims to measure. Thus a test which only asks pupils to identify different types of lighting is easy to administer and straightforward to mark. It is in a technical sense a 'reliable' form of assessment because the room for subjectivity in making judgements is minimised. However, it is not a valid form of assessment because being able to perform this one task is hardly an appropriate judge of ability in drama. Validity and reliability tend to pull in different directions. If a teacher wants to make an assessment which compares Pupil A with Pupil B fairly, the more complex the form of assessment becomes (balancing judgements on attainment targets and strands, individual and group work, written responses, pupil self-evaluations, pupils' logs, etc.) the more difficult this task is.

At Key Stage 4 the assessment process will largely be driven by the demands of external examinations. In the context of English, the National Curriculum is likely to determine the approach. When drama is taught as a separate subject a system needs to be established which is operable without being too reductive. Assessing pupils at the end of each half-termly project is likely to be more workable than trying to complete complex grids for each pupil for every single lesson. If schemes of work have been devised to culminate in a piece of work with specific criteria (based on 'making' or 'responding' or both) this reduces the pressure at other times when the teacher can concentrate on more formative assessment. Direct observation of pupils' drama work can be supplemented by their own oral or written reflections. As with planning drama, it is important that assessment takes account of both content and form: not 'demonstrate a variety of dramatic forms' but 'demonstrate a variety of dramatic forms which explore and communicate ideas with subtlety and depth'. The further reading section at the end of this chapter provides details of publications with lists of assessment criteria and examples of assessment grids.

Recording work

It is important that pupils themselves have a sense of progression in the subject. One of the problems with placing the focus entirely on the learning and understanding which results from participation in drama is that the experiences can feel somewhat ephemeral, and progress rather static. Drama can provide some of the most powerful and enriching experiences for pupils but by its nature does not leave lasting records. The problem here facing drama teachers is similar to that with which English teachers have to contend in the context of oral work when actual records other than teacher's judgements are required for the purposes of external assessment. There are two concerns here. One is to provide records to corroborate assessment, the other is to provide pupils with a lasting record of their achievements.

Video-recordings of workshop sessions as well as finished products are important not just in providing pupils with a record and a focus for analysis and discussion but in allowing the shared negotiation among teachers of what counts as quality with respect to drama. Other methods of recording work can provide a focus for accumulating evidence of achievement and providing a lasting record:

■ audio-recordings, including those which are made to use within drama (e.g. news announcements, interviews, documentaries) and of reflections after the drama;

■ course diaries in which participants reflect on the drama in which they have been engaged and their own individual contributions;

■ related written work – posters, letters in role, historical documents;

- reviews of plays watched and any theatre visits;
- photographs of tableaux and key moments in plays;
- diagrams of the way space was used to construct drama;
- records of research undertaken in order to inform the drama (e.g. interviews with relatives on the theme of immigration).

At every Key Stage the type of sharing and 'trial marking' in which standards are discussed and agreed (a procedure with which GCSE teachers are familiar) are needed. It is a false hope to expect to establish completely objective criteria for describing progress and for assessment purposes; language is not precise enough an instrument to achieve that goal. What is needed is a sharing of subjective judgements as to what counts as quality of achievement in the subject.

Further reading

For discussions of progression and achievement in drama see Arts Council (2003) *Drama in Schools*, Kempe, A. and Ashwell, M. (2000) *Progression in Secondary Drama*, Hornbrook, D. (1991) *Education in Drama*, chapter 6; Bolton, G. (1992a) *New Perspectives on Classroom Drama*, chapter 7. Drama books which present specific courses include Bennathan, J. (2000) *Developing Drama Skills*, O'Toole, J. and Haseman, B (1987) *Dramawise*, Kempe, A. (1990a) *The GCSE Drama Coursebook*, Linnell, R. (1988) *Practical Drama Handbook*.

10

Conclusion

Drama and art

WHEN I WAS A PUPIL in junior school many years ago I can recall standing with a group of friends during open day looking at the art work on the walls. Everyone was busy spotting their own contribution to the display and my friends asked me whether any of the paintings was mine. In good faith I showed them a splendid picture of a daffodil coloured in vivid yellows and greens and carefully shaded. They were suitably impressed and I enjoyed the adulation. This lasted only moments, however, because just then the real author of the piece came along and claimed the work as his own by pointing out his initials in the corner; I had unwittingly picked the wrong painting. My friends rather gleefully set about locating my daffodil and we found it on a wall around the corner looking like an upturned custard pie stuck on the end of a knitting needle. I recognised it as mine and at that moment it seemed impossible to have mistaken one for the other, such was the difference between the two pieces of work. From the point of view of art education, however, did it matter what the product looked like, given that the experience of painting the daffodil, the process in which I had been involved, had been significant enough for me to have thought I painted the first one?

Well, it did to me, and years later I can recall the feelings of embarrassment I suffered at the time. The question posed in relation to the anecdote highlights a central dichotomy which has a long legacy in art and drama education which is encaptured in such contrasting notions as 'subjectivity' and 'objectivity', 'private' and 'public' domains. If the justification for art is based on ideas of individual self-expression and creativity, on what it felt at the moment of creating the art work, then it matters little what the daffodil actually looked like. But common sense and the memories of an eleven-year-old confirm that it does matter; ideas of objective standards and public criteria are significant and in practice intrude irrespective of the theoretical foundation on which art education is based. On the other hand, from an educational point of view, many would argue that the circumstances of the creation of the piece do have some significance: whether, for example, its author was painting by numbers, copying a drawing from a book, or engaged in a genuine aesthetic experience. In the context of drama in which the concepts of process and product are more closely entwined, the problem is more acute as was discussed in Chapter 1. To put the question very simply: in the creation of drama is it the experience and feeling of the participants which matters more or the way the work looks to an outsider? This will be a central question in this final chapter.

One of the aims of this book has been to provide an introduction to the teaching of drama as both separate subject and as an integrated part of the curriculum. As argued in the Introduction, an understanding of the importance and interrelationship of theory and practice is necessary if drama is to be seen as anything more than just an entertaining diversion from the real business of learning in schools. As suggested in Chapter 1 in the context of a discussion of the history of the subject, drama teaching in schools needs to build on the progress and successes of the past, particularly on the considerable advances forged by exponents of drama in education. That view needs further exploration, in relation to the dilemma identified above.

It is not easy to say in any definitive sense what the category 'drama in education' stands for. Simplistic assumptions that drama in education means being anti-theatre, or being dedicated only to one methodology of spontaneous improvisation, or that it refers exclusively to the use of drama across the curriculum, do not stand close scrutiny and do not tend to be advanced now. One of the major contributions made by exponents of drama in education was the new emphasis on content. Bolton (1998) makes this clear in his history of the subject. Previous exponents of drama teaching conceived the subject in different ways: as mime, acting out stories, as a form of amateur dramatics, as speech training, movement, dramatic playing. Heathcote, however, placed a major emphasis on meaning and content. Instead of practising walking like a king, dressing up in a king's robes, miming a crowning ceremony and so on, a pupil in a drama in education lesson might have examined such areas as how a king copes with the responsibilities of power, the loneliness of being a king, knowing who to trust. That does not mean that the sorts of physical activities and exercises described might not figure in a lesson but they would be a means to an end rather than the end itself. The other emphasis in drama in education was on the quality of the experience of the participants. This view had its origins in the work of earlier writers and it is an area which has caused frequent confusion.

Slade and Way used terms such as 'absorption' and 'sincerity' to highlight this as a priority. Later writers used concepts such as 'raw emotion', 'living through experiences' and 'gut feeling'. As often when a new wave of thinking responds to the inadequacies of a previous age, too much of a corrective emphasis was given.

As a reaction against what was seen as the superficial approach to drama which asked pupils to engage in exercises without much sense of purpose ('walk like a king . . . bow to your subjects . . . wave your hand'), many teachers now saw the purpose of drama as being the stirring up of 'real' feelings. Drama workshops were often judged to be successful by the degree to which participants claimed to have been really moved by the experience. This was the 'how was it for you?' approach to drama which placed considerable power in the hands of the participants and much less in those of the hapless group leader who could be told dismissively 'I didn't feel a thing'. But this was a reaction against a form of practice which only recognised as important the external form of the action. However, it does not take much reflection to see that the extremes described here are not tenable. As Stanislavski recognised, contrary to the way his work is often represented, 'sometimes it is possible to arrive at the inner characteristics of a part by way of its outer characteristics' (quoted in Mitter 1992: 17). It is not always possible to separate external action from feeling. A child may pretend to cry in order to have his way and become genuinely upset in the process. A participant in drama may have the intention to pretend to be very angry and end up feeling angry in the process. At the other extreme it makes little sense to claim that participants experience the same feeling when they are engaged in a make-believe that they would in the equivalent experience in real life.

A closely related dichotomy which was discussed in Chapter 8 is that between 'acting' or 'appearing to be' as opposed to 'experiencing'. As pointed out in that discussion, the distinction becomes complicated when it is realised that 'acting' itself is a concept which has different interpretations and meanings. Here, for example, is Stanislavski (1926: 25) comparing different traditions of acting:

> According to the mechanical actor the object of theatrical speech and plastic movements – as exaggerated sweetness in lyric movements, dull monotone in reading epic poetry, hissing sounds to express hatred, false tears in the voice to express grief – is to enhance voice, diction and movements, to make actors more beautiful and give more power to their theatrical effectiveness. Unfortunately . . . in place of nobility a sort of showiness has been created, prettiness in place of beauty, theatrical effect in place of expressiveness.

Leaving aside the difficulties raised by the use of terms like 'acting', the contrast centred on the surface appearance of the action as opposed to the inner experience of the participants. This contrast between the 'internal' and 'external' has been a key feature of describing developments in drama teaching. The emphasis on 'internal' dimensions of experience, on the nature of the feeling of the participants, has been the target for criticism by some of the detractors of the tradition of drama in education. It has been vulnerable to criticism that it has, under the influence of Romanticism, internalised art, changing the emphasis from craft and production to vague notions of subjectivity and authentic expression. Hornbrook (1989: 69) has argued that the two forces of nineteenth-century Romanticism and twentieth-century developmental psychology conspired to shape post-war thinking about art education. '. . . It was these two powerful forces that turned us away from thinking of art as a matter of making and appraising socially valued products, and towards the idea of art as a therapeutic engagement with the inner world of individuals.' He goes on to suggest that the traditional hostility to public performance was accompanied by 'an unwillingness to disengage from' an 'overriding commitment to personal feeling response' (*ibid*.: 71).

It would appear then that drama teachers are faced with a choice between a theoretical model which relies on valuing such concepts as 'subjectivity', 'engagement', 'significance', 'depth' as opposed to one which values external manifestations of behaviour, that which is objective and visible. The problem, however, with theoretical discussions which are too far removed from practicalities is that they force choices which do not bear any proper relation to our actual experiences. Drama teachers know (although they may not use this terminology) that a concept of internal action does have some significance, for a lesson based simply on getting the actions right would offer little by way of artistic or educational experience. It was this emphasis on the quality of the experience of the participants in the drama with which the work of Bolton and Heathcote is closely associated. At the start of Way's *Development Through Drama* the author, in a frequently quoted passage, used the example of 'blindness' to evoke the power of drama as an experiential form of learning:

> The answer to many simple questions might take one of two forms – either that of information or else that of direct experience; the former answer belongs to the category of academic education, the latter to drama. For example, the question might be 'What is a blind person?' The reply could be 'A blind person is a person who cannot see'. Alternatively, the reply could be 'Close your eyes and, keeping them closed all the time, try to find your way out of this room.' The first answer contains concise and accurate information; the mind is possibly satisfied. But the second answer leads the inquirer to moments of direct experience, transcending mere knowledge, enriching the imagination, possibly touching the heart and soul as well as the mind. This, in over-simplified terms, is the precise function of drama.
>
> (Way 1967: 1)

It was in 1976 that Bolton challenged whether this exercise would in itself do much to enhance the participants' understanding of blindness:

> The exercise, while useful in giving the participant a crude understanding of visual deprivation, needs to be extended considerably if the concept of blindness is to be tackled seriously. Indeed if it is to move onto a plane of drama rather than remain as an exercise, restricting the sense must somehow acquire a symbolic meaning beyond the immediate sense experience.
>
> (Bolton 1976)

Hornbrook (1989: 92) makes a similar comment, 'Does closing our eyes and walking across the room, for example, really allow us to perceive the world as a blind person does?'

The key point here is not that the physical exercise is of no value but that it is not in itself sufficient for developing a drama about blindness. It might be a valuable starting point, just as a number of lessons described in Chapter 9 started with games or physical activity of some kind. An equally valid starting point for a lesson dealing with the theme of blindness might be to engage the pupils in a discussion of the issue or to read an extract from a play text. It is possible to work in drama from the 'inside out' or from the 'outside in' as demonstrated in the following quotations from Brook and Stanislavski (Mitter 1992: 6).

> The actor must dig inside himself for responses, but at the same time must be open to outside stimuli. Acting was the marriage of these two processes.

> Actually in each physical act there is an inner psychological motive which impels physical action, as in every psychological inner action there is also a physical action, which expresses its psychic nature. The union of these two actions results in organic action on the stage.

Once again, theory needs to be grounded in practice if sense is to be made of either. To base an argument on a strict division between what is 'internal' and 'external' is to take language too seriously, is to fail to recognise that the relationship between language and reality is complex and that we use terms like 'internal' and 'external' as approximations, as metaphors, to make sense of our lives and experiences. To attempt to disinfect language and accounts of drama and art of references to subjectivity, authenticity and feeling is to provide more superficially attractive, 'rational' explanations which, however, are ultimately reductive because they leave out much that is important. That is not to say that many criticisms of art as self-expression are not valid. However, a closer examination of the sort of reservations voiced in the context of aesthetics about this particular theory reveals the degree to which the misconception underlying such accounts of art rests on a misunderstanding of the nature of feeling and emotion. These misunderstandings in turn are derived from a mistaken view of the way language works.

Self-expression

Self-expression theories of art, as the title suggests, concentrated attention on what was said to be going on in the process of creation: the artist is said to be expressing inner feeling or emotions in the work of art. Osborne (1968: 132) places such views in their historical context, embodying, as he has pointed out, the prevailing mood of romanticism:

> . . . the elevation of the artist; the exaltation of originality; the new value set on experience as such with a special emphasis on the affective and emotional aspects of experience; and the new importance attached to fiction and invention.

A number of arguments are traditionally advanced against self-expression theories. An examination of the actual way artists work produces certain problems. What we know of the creative process suggests that it is by no means clear that it follows the pattern suggested by the theory, of 'solitary geniuses engaged in mysterious acts of self-expression' (Hospers 1954–55). It has been recognised that great art has been produced by people who would not testify to being caught in the throes of creation, who may have been motivated as much by the desire to make money or to perfect their craft as they have to the urge to give expression to emotions. If self-expression is used as a criterion for evaluation we have to contend with those cases in which people might claim to have experienced strong emotions in the act of creation but have produced nothing resembling art. Self-expression theories can be viewed as extreme forms of the 'intentional fallacy' in which the feelings and intentions of the artist are supreme.

These then are some of the telling criticisms which have been advanced against the explanation of art as self-expression. However, another type of challenge derives from the view of emotion implicit in the theory and is of relevance to the discussion of 'internal' and 'external' dimensions of human activity. What the theory rests on is a view of emotion which sees it as some 'inner turbulence', an occurrence in a private world which overflows and finds expression in the particular art form. Language deceives us into thinking that words which relate to feelings, motives, and even personal characteristics are identifying some mysterious internal entity which is somehow separate from the 'external' actions in which they appear to find expression. The point is not to argue that emotions are not felt as sensations (for that would be to deny an obvious fact of our existence that when someone is angry they can undergo actual physical changes) but to see that it is not an adequate explanation of *what such words mean* to claim that they are simply referring to an 'inner' sensation. If emotions were merely sensations it would make no sense to talk about them being directed at particular people or objects. Nor would it make sense to talk about emotions being reasonable or unreasonable, although that is precisely the way we do talk about them. Do we distinguish a concept like 'indignation' from 'annoyance' by examining the different twinge or inner sensation caused by each? The answer is clearly that we do not. The distinguishing factor is the context which gave rise to the particular feelings. If my car breaks down because it has run out of petrol it makes little sense to say I am indignant because that term carries connotations that someone has reneged on their duty; it would only be appropriate if, for example, the garage mechanic had failed to fill the tank as requested after a service (Bedford 1956: 292).

An emotion is what it is, not simply by virtue of its intrinsic characteristics as a feeling but also by virtue of its relationship to its object and to its situation. Of course the same arguments which are used to deny the ideas that descriptions of emotions and feelings are explanations of private inner states can also be used to show the inadequacy of an extreme behaviourist view which sees external manifestations of behaviour as being all that matters. For in that case it would not be possible to make any distinction between real emotions and pretence. We discover that someone was pretending to be angry by subsequent information derived from the context, not by examining their internal state to see if their anger was genuine. More tellingly, an explanation of this kind does not actually accord with what it feels like to be in a particular state of feeling or emotion.

Midgley (1979: 106), while discussing behaviourist attempts to describe the outer manifestations of behaviour alone, makes the point that most of the terms in which we can describe behaviour effectively do refer to the *experience* of the agent as well.

> Reference to a conscious subject always slips in, whatever the disinfecting precautions, simply because language has been so framed as to carry it.

She goes on to say that descriptions of human activities like laughing or crying are not just describing standard outward movement any more than they are just describing states of mind but such movements made with certain sorts of feelings or intentions.

She takes the case of laughter to make her point in more detail. From an external point of view laughing is just making a strange noise similar to one which might be made by a physical subject like a saw or an animal like a hyena. The noise itself, however, is not what we would want to describe as a laugh. Moreover, it makes perfect sense for someone to say 'they were all laughing at me' even though no noise has been made and the speaker has been treated with outward politeness by those he is accusing. Midgley continues as follows:

> If we want to understand such notion, there is no substitute for grasping the kind of subjective, conscious state in which such noises are typically made, and for this you need to be capable of something like it yourself. Someone who does not grasp that state at all will be simply unable to recognise a laugh – to distinguish it reliably from coughs, sobs, snorts, and other noises – let alone to interpret its point and meaning.

This discussion can now be related to the concepts of 'internal' and 'external' action. The mistake against which drama teachers need to guard is not to avoid the use of such terms but to avoid the assumption that it is possible to explain human behaviour by virtue of one of them alone:

> ... there would certainly be trouble if we were forced to choose between describing outer actions and inner experience – if we could not have both. But we do have both. People have insides as well as outsides; they are subjects as well as objects. And these two aspects operate together. We need views on both to make sense of either. And, normally, both are included in all descriptions of behaviour.
>
> (*ibid.*: 112)

It may seem as if the discussion has moved away from the practical realities of the classroom but that is far from the case. When we judge the quality of a piece of drama, logic tells us that we can only do so by judging what we see. But in doing so it is perfectly legitimate to make inferences about the depth of engagement and the evident understanding of content. Indeed it is only necessary to think of extreme examples to realise that is precisely what we do in the classroom. If groups in drama have been asked to prepare and perform a scene about a shipwreck and they have an uproarious time jumping in and out of the water escaping from sharks, it is safe to claim that this is not good drama and part of what we are doing in forming that judgement is making an inference about the attitude of the participants. Similarly a group who perform their scene about a shipwreck and appear 'stagey', over-drilled, mechanical, devoid of any genuine commitment or understanding can likewise be judged not to have produced drama of quality. Notice that talk of 'quality' in relation to drama necessarily involves attention to feeling *and* content. This is exactly what is to be expected from the theoretical discussion which showed that feeling is always what it is by virtue of its relationship with an object.

A mistake made by drama practitioners in the past was to assume that there is a necessary causal connection between particular methodologies in drama and work of quality. But a class who are experienced and competent in the subject (and this is a key factor) should be able to produce quality work even on the basis of the once discredited 'get into groups and do a play' approach. Nor is this a departure from the notion of 'drama as learning', if, as argued in Chapter 2, the process of formulation embodied in the idea of 'expression' is seen as central. However, it would be equally mistaken to assume that simply telling a group to act out a scene, or 'training' them in various drama skills, will produce work of quality. One of the contributions made by pioneers like Heathcote and Bolton has been to develop drama teaching methods, many of which have been described in this book, designed to further that aim. This discussion also underlines the importance of context and process in making judgements about pupils' drama work.

Drama and experience

Because it is important to preserve notions of the 'inner' and 'outer' dimensions of experience the argument advanced by States (1985) of the importance of a 'binocular vision', which embraces semiotics and phenomenology as complementary perspectives on the world and art, is attractive. Semiotics is defined as a 'science dedicated to the study of the production of meaning in society' (Elam 1980: 1). It has made an invaluable contribution to the study of theatre and drama by opening up ways of seeing how drama works, of how theatrical performances use signs to create meaning. As described by States (1985: 6) it sees theatre 'as a process of mediation between artist and culture, speaker and listener; theatre becomes a passageway for a cargo of meanings being carried back to society (after artistic refinement) via the language of signs.' Semiotics concentrates attention on the way sign systems of drama (words, expression, gesture, lighting, music and so on) combine to communicate meaning to an audience: 'the full meaning of dramatic performance must of necessity always emerge from the total impact of these complex, multi-layered structures of interwoven and independent signifiers' (Esslin 1987: 106).

While States acknowledges the value of the semiotic enterprise, he points out the danger of neglecting to recognise the importance of our 'sensory engagement' with the theatre. Attention to structures and signs focuses attention on what might be termed 'objective' dimensions but does not describe the experiences of the participants in the enterprise.

> If we think of semiotics and phenomenology as modes of seeing, we might say that they constitute a kind of binocular vision: one eye enables us to see the world phenomenally; the other eye enables us to see it significatively. These are the abnormal extremes of our normal vision.'
>
> (States 1985: 8)

Phenomenology has been employed by writers on drama in education in the past but its theoretical influence as a way of thinking about the world has met with resistance because of its associations with a total system of thought. It is anathema to some writers because of its associations with extreme forms of subjectivism and idealism. However, if phenomenology is seen not as a total 'philosophy' in a broad sense but as a reflection on experience then one can see its value in balancing a perspective which only concentrates on objective, external appearances. When pupils are engaged in creating or observing drama, the quality of their experience, which is a function of their understanding and 'feeling-response' is important, as is their manipulation of signs to create meaning. That is why teaching drama is itself a delicate art which balances two extremes – avoiding the kind of indulgent, non-discerning approach which has rightly been criticised by Hornbrook but also eschewing a return to mere 'show', to what Davis (1991) has described as 'the days when prop cupboards were the order of the day and the children dressed up and "acted" the part'. The placing of the word 'acted' in inverted commas demonstrates that it is not the use of the term which is important but what it means in practice.

Once again, as has frequently been the case in this book, the discussion centres on language and the effect it has on our thinking. It is important to recognise the power of language but also to acknowledge its sometimes disruptive effects. As suggested earlier, words like 'internal' and 'external' experience imply that these are distinct entities between which we have to choose, rather than constructs or metaphors which are most usefully seen as complementary concepts. A work by New York artist John Spinks has as one of its themes the relationship between language and that which it depicts. In the middle of the canvas on either side of a central dividing line are two small words no more than half a centimetre high in lower case letters. They have obviously been cut out from a book. The words themselves are what they depict, 'two' and 'words'. The central dividing line which is raised from the canvas can now be recognised as the spine of an old book and the two faded blank pages the background for the words which have been inserted on it. The symmetry and colour of the piece with its delicate, faded texture is very satisfying but it is also thought-provoking. At one level, because it is so understated, the work seems to be giving a literal view of language and meaning: we see two words and we read 'two words': the relationship between sign and signifier is uncomplicated. Yet the work also reminds us that meaning is rarely that transparent. The context (this is an old book with only two words on the pages) undercuts its own simple interpretation of the language, inviting speculation not only about the resonance of the concept of 'word' itself ('in the beginning was the word') but about meaning (does the printed word have a future in our technological society?): 'two words' means more than 'two words'. What is also interesting about the piece is that although it invites us to think cognitively and conceptually, its meaning is not circumscribed by that process.

There is an important parallel here with drama. It is sometimes assumed that because we are dealing with an art form it is not appropriate to speak about 'learning' which comes about as a result of engagement in drama; this point was introduced in Chapter 2. However, once we recognise that any formulation in language with respect to learning outcomes in drama can only ever be an indication of priority and emphasis, the way is paved for more constructive talk about educational purpose. Nor is the intention of the author the factor which alone determines meaning. Just as in the case of the work of art it is legitimate to speculate on what the piece means irrespective of the precise intentions, one of the teacher's tasks in the drama lesson is to help pupils understand and respond to what may have been created intuitively. Much of the power of drama resides in the way ambiguities, tensions and the multi-layered meanings of its language and other sign systems are explored.

It would be ironic therefore if the theory and practice of drama (which itself needs to operate successfully by balancing opposing tensions) becomes reductive, and certain, disinfecting it of those crucial elements which make it an essentially human enterprise. It is a superficially attractive view fostered by certain views of language itself that we can 'disengage from our world by objectifying it' (Taylor 1985: 4). The value of drama is that it invites people to make connections with their world, to understand and to challenge it.

It is fitting that a book on *Starting Drama Teaching* should not end conclusively despite the title of this chapter. Tension which is at the heart of creating drama is also at the centre of thinking about its processes and it would be unwise to look for easy solutions to all the theoretical and practical problems it presents.

Further reading

For discussions of issues related to aesthetics see Lyas, C. (1997) *Aesthetics*, Hanfling, O. (1992) *Philosophical Aesthetics*, Cooper, D. (1992) *A Companion to Aesthetics* and Eaton, M. (1988) *Basic Issues in Aesthetics*. Warburton, N. (1992) *Philosophy – the Basics* has a chapter on dualism. Further reading on this topic can be found in Hammond, M. *et al.* (1991) *Understanding Phenomenology* and Cooper, D. (1990) *Existentialism – A Reconstruction*. See Taylor, C. (ed.) (1996) *Researching Drama and Arts Education* for chapters on drama and research.

The doctor's visit

THIS TRANSCRIPT IS A VERBATIM RECORD of a period of sustained drama involving an adult and a child of four years of age. The child had previously been ill and during the first part of the exchange is coming to terms with his own experiences. As the drama develops he moves outside the sphere of his own recent encounters to explore concepts of death and burial. Extracts from the text were used in Chapter 2 to illustrate the way in which art can bring us closer to human life experiences, in Chapter 5 to explore distinctions between 'play' and 'drama', in Chapter 6 to show how easily a young child can move in and out of role, and in Chapter 9 in order to highlight the difficulties involved in describing progression in drama. One of the themes throughout this book has been the way false assumptions about the relationship of language to thought and reality have misleading consequences. The transcript provides an insight into the child's grasp of concepts in relation to his use of language. Comments on the action outside the drama are given in italics.

(CHILD: *This is my 'phone isn't it?*)

ADULT: Hello.

CHILD: Hello.

ADULT: Hello. Doctor would you come over? My little boy is not well. He's got a swelling on his neck. Could you come over right away?

CHILD: Yes. Bye.

ADULT: Bye.

(CHILD: *Then you tell the little boy okay – go on then.*)

ADULT: The doctor's coming over now and I want you to be good. I don't want you to be naughty when he comes.

(CHILD: *Then you be the little boy. You say 'Quick get into bed because the doctor is coming'.*)

ADULT: Quick get into bed the doctor's coming. Here he is – there's a knock on the door. (*Sound of knocking*)

ADULT: Oh! Come in doctor. He's in here on the settee.

CHILD: Hello.

ADULT: Hello.

(Pause as doctor opens his bag)

CHILD: Open up your mouth. Open up your mouth. Let me see what's in it . . . Thank you . . . Right, we're not going to have an injection. Give us your ear. *(Patient laughs as if tickled)* It's got a light in it to see what's inside your ear. *(Laughter from patient as if tickled)* Right I'll have to give you some medicine.

ADULT: Does it taste nasty?

CHILD: No, it's very nice – my children like it.

ADULT: Do they?

CHILD: It is nice? See I told you it would be nice. I saw a little cut on your ear so I have to put a bandage on. There you go. You have to stay in bed and stay off nursery okay . . . with your mummy and play soft games.

[The child seems to be clearly imitating recent experiences in order to come to terms with them. His insistence that 'we're not going to have an injection' is no doubt a projection of what he would wish in a similar situation. Notice that he appears to have a sophisticated grasp of medical procedures when he examines the ear only to reveal subsequently that he has been looking for a cut – logical enough when you are four years old.]

ADULT: Why soft games?

CHILD: Because you might get poorly.

ADULT: What game can't I play?

CHILD: Like Bat-man and He-man.

ADULT: And what games can I play?

CHILD: Like Lego, that's a good game isn't it and you can play with your stickers.

ADULT: Can I go swimming?

CHILD: No, you have to stay off. You can tell your mummy bye bye. Go and tell your mummy please.

ADULT: What shall I tell her?

CHILD: That you have to stay off nursery okay and swimming baths.

ADULT: Will you tell her?

CHILD: No, you can tell her. 'Cos I'm going now. Bye.

ADULT: Bye.

CHILD: You tell your mummy okay.

ADULT: Mum. I have to stay off nursery. Yes. Doctor said.

(CHILD: Tomorrow you're very, very poorly okay.)

(ADULT: Right, I'll be very poorly. This time I can't even talk. You have to try and make me talk.)

(Phone rings)

ADULT: Doctor.

CHILD: Hello.

ADULT: My little boy is worse today. He's very poorly.

CHILD: What happened to him?

ADULT: Well I don't know, he's hardly talking. He's not eating anything.

CHILD: Can he not talk properly?

ADULT: No.

CHILD: Oh! Right I'll be on my way.

ADULT: Thank you. Come straight in. He's in his bed.

CHILD: Okay.

(Ding dong)

(CHILD: The mummy comes to open the door.)

ADULT: Come on doctor this way. He's in here.

CHILD: Are you all right? Cough please. (ADULT coughs)

CHILD: Open your mouth. Oh it's measles. It's measles. Now you can close. I'm the doctor. Your temperature's higher today 'cos look. Don't cry. Don't cry. You'll soon be better.

[The child's assertion 'I'm the doctor', which is unnecessary for the make-believe, is an indication that he is holding both the real and the fictitious context in his mind at the same time. The statement reveals that he knows he is not the doctor – he is declaring his part in the drama. His diagnosis follows its own logic even though it bears no relation to medical reality; he is developing a concept of diagnosis by asserting his own logic.]

(CHILD: The next day you can't even cry. Okay. The next day you can't even cry.)

CHILD: You have to have an injection. Put your sleeve up please . . . I'm just taking away all that blood.

(Draws on syringe)

ADULT: Don't want an injection.

(CHILD: I thought you can't talk.)

CHILD: You have to take an injection. Don't cry. Don't cry. Don't shut your mouth. We have to put a bandage on it. *(Pause)* There it's finished. Will you ask your mummy to put a plaster on it when you get home please? Okay. Go on then. Tell your mummy to put a plaster on it okay. *(Pause)* Tell your mummy to put a plaster on it. Bye bye.

ADULT: Bye bye see you.

(CHILD: You're worsen tomorrow. You're the mummy now.)

(Phone rings)

ADULT: Doctor, doctor – come over quickly. My little boy he doesn't even have his eyes open.

CHILD: I'll be on my way quickly.

ADULT: Good, thank you . . . This way doctor he's in here quick, quick.

CHILD: It's me the doctor. Pull your sleeve. *(Pause)* Mother, mother, mother. He's dead.

[Notice that it is the child not the adult who introduces the idea of death; the drama is taking him beyond his recent experiences. At the start of this exchange we realise that the child assumes that an injection is to remove blood – again, a logical enough deduction for a four-year-old but earlier we might have thought he had a more developed concept by virtue of his use of language.]

ADULT: Oh no. *(Cries)* What are we going to do now?
CHILD: Take him . . . Let's call the ambulance.
ADULT: What good will calling an ambulance do?
CHILD: Make him better.
ADULT: But I thought you said he was dead.
CHILD: Yes but then you'll make him better.
(CHILD: *Then you 'phone up. Then you be the nurse okay.)*
CHILD: Hello, is the nurse calling?
ADULT: Yes this is the nurse at the hospital. What can I do for you?
CHILD: I'm at somebody's house. She had a little boy who's dead. Will you come and fix him up please?

[Now we discover that his concept of death is not fully developed.]

ADULT: Well there's nothing much I can do. You'll just have to get him buried.
CHILD: Oh. Bye, bye.
ADULT: Bye, bye.
CHILD : Mother.
ADULT : Yes. *(Cries)*
CHILD : We'll just have to get him buried. There's nothing the nurse can do about it.
ADULT : Well, how do you do that? What do you mean bury him?
CHILD : We put a cross up. I've got a cross in my doctor's house here. We have to put a cross and put his name. What's his name?
ADULT : His name is David.
CHILD : So we have to put David, okay. Come on, we just have to bury him.
(CHILD: *Then you be the little boy.)*
ADULT : But I'm going to be sad now.
CHILD : We'll just have to bury him.
ADULT: But I'm going to be so sad.

[The adult is more interested in the emotional aspects of the situation than the child who proceeds to demonstrate now that he has more of a concept of death than we had previously thought.]

CHILD : You're the little boy.
(Sound and action of digging)
CHILD : David. *(Writing on cross)*

(CHILD: *You talk as a little boy okay, with your eyes open 'cos you come alive again. You say that you're under the ground.*)

ADULT: Hey let me out. Let me out.

CHILD: Hey it's you.

ADULT: What was I doing down there with all that earth on me?

CHILD: We thought you were dead.

ADULT: I feel a bit better now.

CHILD: Let's go back in my doctor's car okay.

(*Sound of driving*)

CHILD: Are you all right back there?

ADULT: Are you going to take me back to my mum? (*Sound of driving*) What's she doing – is she sad?

CHILD: Here you are. Let's go in your house. Say hello to your mummy.

ADULT: Hello mummy. I'm better.

(CHILD: *Make your mummy talk.* ADULT: *Do you want to be the mummy?*)

CHILD: Hello.

ADULT: I'm better.

CHILD: How nice to see you. (*Hugs*) I just bought a little present for you while I was out.

ADULT: Did you?

CHILD: Yes.

ADULT: Oh good. What is it?

CHILD: Close your eyes. Now you can open them.

ADULT: What is it? Oh, it's a doctor's kit.

CHILD: I bought it for you.

ADULT: And can I play doctors?

CHILD: Yes.

ADULT: And will you be the patient?

CHILD: Yes.

ADULT: Good.

CHILD: Shall we play that later?

ADULT: Yes.

[The drama finishes with a self-referential ending which gives it a satisfying unity. The boy and the adult in the fiction will later play doctors just as the boy and the adult did in reality to initiate the drama.]

Bibliography

Abbs, P. (1992) 'Abbs Replies to Bolton', *Drama*, Summer, 1(1), 2–6.

Ackroyd, J. (2000) *Literacy Alive*. London: Hodder & Stoughton.

Adams, C. and Sullivan, M. (1982) *The Evacuees*. Surrey: Youngsong Music.

Alington, A. (1961) *Drama and Education*. Oxford: Basil Blackwell.

Allen, J. (1979) *Drama in Schools: Its Theory and Practice*. London: Heinemann.

Arts Council of Great Britain (2003) *Drama in Schools*. London: Arts Council. First edition published in 1992.

Aston, E. and Savona, G. (1991) *Theatre as Sign-system*. London: Routledge.

Baldwin, P. (1991) *Stimulating Drama – Cross-Curricular Approaches to Drama in the Primary School*. Norwich: Norwich County Council.

Baldwin, P. and Fleming, K. (2003) *Teaching Literacy Through Drama*. London:Routledge/Falmer.

Banks, R. A. (1991) *Drama and Theatre Arts*. London: Hodder & Stoughton.

Barker, C. (1977) *Theatre Games: A New Approach to Drama Training*. London: Methuen.

Barlow, S. and Skidmore, S. (1994) *Dramaform – A Practical Guide to Drama Techniques*. London: Hodder & Stoughton.

Barthes, R. (1977) *Image, Music, Text*. London: Fontana.

Battye, S. (1993) 'Examining Dramatic Art', *2D*, Spring, 1(2).

Bedford, E. (1956) 'Emotions', *Proceedings of the Aristotelian Society*, 1956–57, supplement LVII, 281–303.

Bennathan, J. (2000) *Developing Drama Skills*. London: Heinemann.

Bennett, S. (1984) 'Drama: The Practice of Freedom', National Association for the Teaching of Drama third annual lecture, 12 November. London: NATD.

Bennett, S. (1990) *Theatre Audiences: A Theory of Production and Reception*. London: Routledge.

Berry, C. (1993) *The Actor and the Text*. London: Virgin Books. Revised edition.

Best, D. (1992) *The Rationality of Feeling*. London: The Falmer Press.

Boal, A. (1992) *Games for Actors and Non-Actors* (translated by A. Jackson). London: Routledge.

Bolton, G. (1976) 'Drama as Metaphor', *Young Drama*, 4(3), June, reprinted in Davis, D. and Lawrence, C. (1986) *Gavin Bolton: Selected Writings*. London: Longman, 42–7.

Bolton, G. (1979) *Towards a Theory of Drama in Education*. London: Longman.

Bolton, G. (1984) *Drama as Education*. London: Longman.

Bolton, G. (1990) 'Opinion – Education and Dramatic Art – A Review', *Drama Broadsheet*, Spring, 7(1), 2–5.

Bolton, G. (1992a) *New Perspectives on Classroom Drama*. Hemel Hempstead: Simon & Schuster.

Bolton, G. (1992b) 'Have a Heart', *Drama*, Summer, 1(1), 7–8.

Bolton, G. (1998) *Acting in Classroom Drama*. Stoke-on-Trent: Trentham Books.

Bolton, G. and Heathcote, D. (1999) *So You Want to Use Role Play?* Stoke-on-Trent: Trentham Books.

Bond, T. (1986) *Games for Social and Life Skills*. London: Hutchinson.

Boomer, G. (1984) 'The Politics of Drama Teaching', in Meek, M. and Miller, J. (eds) (1984) *Changing English – Essays for Harold Rosen*. London: Heinemann, 143–54.

Booth, D. (1985) 'To Intervene is to Teach', *Drama Broadsheet*, Summer, 3(3), 10–13.

Booth, D. (1989) 'Imaginary Gardens with Real Toads', *Drama Broadsheet*, Summer, 6(2), 2–6.

Bowell, P. and Heap, B. S. (2001) *Planning Process Drama*. London: David Fulton Publishers.

Brandes, D. (1982) *Gamester's Handbook Two*. London: Hutchinson.

Brandes, D. and Phillips, H. (1978) *Gamester's Handbook*. London: Access Publishing.

Britton, S. (1991) 'The Case for Theatre at the Centre of the Curriculum', *2D*, Winter, 11(1), 8–13.

Brook, P. (1968) *The Empty Space*. Harmondsworth: Penguin Books.

Bruner, J. (1971) *Towards a Theory of Instruction*. Cambridge, Mass.: Harvard University Press.

Bryer, T. (1990) 'Dorothy Heathcote's Mantle of the Expert and Rolling Role – A Personal Account of Two Historic Conferences', *Drama Broadsheet*, Winter, 7(3), 2–7.

Burgess, R. and Gaudry, P. (1985) *Time for Drama – A Handbook for Secondary Teachers*. Milton Keynes: Open University Press.

Byron, K. (1984) 'Drama and Narrative Fiction', *2D*, Summer, 3(3), 51–64.

Byron, K. (1986a) *Drama in the English Classroom*. London: Methuen.

Byron, K. (1986b) 'Drama at the Crossroads', *2D*, Autumn, 6(1), 2–15.

Carey, J. (1990) 'Teaching in Role and Classroom Power', *Drama Broadsheet*, 7(2), 2–8.

Casdagli, P. and Gobey, F. with Griffin, C. (1990) *Only Playing, Miss*. Stoke-on-Trent: Trentham Books.

Casdagli, P. and Gobey, F. with Griffin, C. (1992) *Grief*. London: David Fulton Publishers.

Chaplin, A. (1999) *Drama 9–11*. Leamington Spa: Scholastic.

Clark, J. (1989) 'Drama as Schooling? Drama as Education?', *Drama Broadsheet*, Autumn, 6(3), 12–19.

Claxton, G. (1984) *Live and Learn*. London: Harper & Row.

Clegg, D. (1973) 'The Dilemma of Drama in Education', *Theatre Quarterly*, 111(9), 31–42.

Clipson-Boyles, S. (1998) *Drama in Primary English Teaching*. London: David Fulton Publishers.

Cooper, D. (1990) *Existentialism – A Reconstruction*. Oxford: Basil Blackwell.

Cooper, D. (1992) *A Companion to Aesthetics*. Oxford: Basil Blackwell.

Courtney, R. (1968) *Play, Drama and Thought: The Intellectual Background to Drama in Education*. London: Cassell.

Creber, P. (1990) *Thinking Through English*. Milton Keynes: Open University Press.

Cross, D. (1990) 'Leicestershire GCSE Drama: a Syllabus with a Clear Direction', *2D*, Summer, 9(2), 18–24.

Culpin, C. (1992) *The Making of the U.K.* London: Collins.

Curtis, B. and Mays, W. (eds) (1978) *Phenomenology and Education: self-consciousness and its development*. London: Methuen.

Cutler-Gray, D. and Taylor, K. (1991) 'Finding Wings: Video Drama', *The Drama Magazine*, November, 19–21.

Davies, G. (1983) *Practical Primary Drama*. London: Heinemann.

Davis, D. (1985) 'Dorothy Heathcote Interviewed by D. Davis', *2D*, Summer, 4(3), 64–80.

Davis, D. (1991) 'In Defence of Drama in Education', *NATD Broadsheet*, Autumn, 5–10.

Davis, D. and Lawrence, C. (1986) *Gavin Bolton: Selected Writings*. London: Longman.

DES (1967) *Education Survey 2, Drama*. London: HMSO.

DES (1988) *Report of the Committee of Enquiry into the Teaching of English* (The Kingman Report). London: HMSO.

DES (1989) *Drama 5–16*. London: HMSO.

Dodd, N. and Hickson, W. (eds) (1971) *Drama and Theatre in Education*. London: Heinemann.

Dodgson, E. (1984) *Motherland*. London: Heinemann.

Donaldson, M. (1978) *Children's Minds*. London: Fontana.

Donaldson, M. (1992) *Human Minds: An Exploration*. London: Allen Lane.

Downey, M. and Kelly, A. (1979) *Theory and Practice of Education: An Introduction*. London: Harper & Row.

Eaton, M. (1988) *Basic Issues in Aesthetics*. California: Wadsworth Publishing Company.

Eco, U. (1977) 'Semiotics of Theatrical Performance', *The Drama Review*, xxi, (1), 108–17, reprinted in Walder, D. (1990) *Literature in the Modern World*. Oxford: Oxford University Press and Open University Press, 115–22.

Edwards, A. (1990) 'To Preach What I Practise', *2D*, Winter, 10(1), 17–23.

Elam, K. (1980) *The Semiotics of Theatre and Drama*. London: Methuen. Reprinted in 1988 by Routledge.

Entwistle, N. (1987) *Understanding Classroom Learning*. London: Hodder & Stoughton.

Eriksson, S. and Jantzen, C. (1992) 'Still Pictures: Aesthetic Images in Drama', *Drama*, Summer, 1(1) 9–12.

Esslin, M. (1978) *An Anatomy of Drama*. London: Abacus Sphere Books Ltd.

Esslin, M. (1987) *The Field of Drama*. London: Methuen.

Fleming, M. (1997) *The Art of Drama Teaching*. London: David Fulton Publishers.

Fleming, M. (1999) Progression and continuity in the teaching of Drama', *Drama, The Journal of National Drama*, 7(1), 12–18.

Fleming, M. (2001) *Teaching Drama in Primary and Secondary Schools*. London: David Fulton Publishers.

Fortier, M. (1997) *Theory/Theatre: An Introduction*. London: Routledge.

Frost, A. and Yarrow, R. (1990) *Improvisation in Drama*. London: Macmillan.

Garvin, P. (ed.) (1964) *A Prague School Reader on Esthetics, Literary Structure and Style*. Washington, D.C.: Georgetown University Press.

Gibson, R. (1990) *Secondary School Shakespeare*. Cambridge: Cambridge Institute of Education.

Hadley, G. (1992) 'Just think, all this came from that one little map', *2D*, Summer, 11(2), 6–13.

Hahlo, R. and Reynolds, P. (2000) *Dramatic Events: How to Run a Successful Workshop*. London: Faber & Faber.

Hammond, M., Howarth, J. and Keat, R. (1991) *Understanding Phenomenology*. Oxford: Basil Blackwell.

Hanfling, O. (ed.) (1992) *Philosophical Aesthetics: An Introduction*. Oxford: Basil Blackwell and the Open University.

Harrop, J. (1992) *Acting*. London: Routledge.

Haseman, B. (1991) 'Improvisation, process drama and dramatic art', *The Drama Magazine: Journal of National Drama*, July, 19–21.

Hawkes, T. (1977) *Structuralism and Semiotics*. London: Methuen. Reprinted in 1991 by Routledge.

Heathcote, D. (1980) 'Drama as Context', *NATE papers in education*. London: NATE.

Heathcote, D. (1984) 'The Authentic Teacher and the Future', in Johnson, L. and O'Neill, C. (1984) *Dorothy Heathcote: Collected Writings on Education and Drama*. London: Hutchinson, 170–99.

Heathcote, D. and Bolton, G. (1994) *Drama for Learning: An Account of Dorothy Heathcote's 'Mantle of the Expert'*. Portsmouth, N. H.: Heinemann.

Hill, B. (1991)'The Pioneer Museum', *NATD Broadsheet*, Autumn, 11–13.

Hirst, P. (1974) *Knowledge and the Curriculum*. London: Routledge and Kegan Paul.

HMI (1990) *Aspects of Primary Education: The Teaching and Learning of Drama*. London: HMSO.

Holt, M. (ed.) (1987) *Skills and Vocationalism: The Easy Answer*. Milton Keynes: Open University Press.

Hornbrook, D. (1991) *Education in Drama: Casting the Dramatic Curriculum*. London: Falmer Press.

Hornbrook, D. (1998a) *Education and Dramatic Art*. London: Blackwell Education. First edition published in 1989.

Hornbrook, D. (1998b) (ed.) *On the Subject of Drama*. London: Routledge.

Hospers, J. (1954–55) 'The Concept of Artistic Expression', *Proceedings of the Aristotelian Society*, 55, 313–44, reprinted in Hospers, J. (ed.) (1969) *Introductory Readings in Aesthetics*. New York: Free Press.

Hyland, T. (1993) 'Competence, Knowledge and Education', *Journal of Philosophy of Education*, 27(1), 57–68.

James, D. (1993) 'How Drama Can Be Seen to Help Pupils Achieve the Requirements for Writing in the National Curriculum', *2D*, 12(2), 2–15.

Jeffcoate, R. (1992) *Starting English Teaching*. London: Routledge.

Johnson, L. and O'Neill, C. (1984) *Dorothy Heathcote: Collected Writings on Education and Drama*. London: Hutchinson.

Johnstone, K. (1981) *Impro: Improvisation and the Theatre*. London: Methuen.

Jones, J. (1958–59) 'The Two Contexts of Mental Concepts', *Proceedings of the Aristotelian Society*, 32, 105–24.

Kaiserman, P. (1988) 'Assessment Without Compromise', *2D*, Autumn, 8(1), 42–51.

Kempe, A. (1988) *The Drama Sampler*. Oxford: Basil Blackwell.

Kempe, A. (1990a) *The GCSE Drama Coursebook*. Oxford: Basil Blackwell.

Kempe, A. (1990b) 'Odd bedfellows: A Closer Look at Gavin Bolton's Four Aims in Teaching Drama', *The Drama Magazine*, November, 19–20.

Kempe, A, (ed.) (1996) *Drama Education and Special Needs*. Cheltenham: Stanley Thornes.

Kempe, A. and Ashwell, M. (2000) *Progression in Secondary Drama*. London: Heinemann.

Kempe, A. and Holroyd, R. (1993) *Evacuees*. London: Hodder & Stoughton.

Kempe, A. and Nicholson, H. (2001) *Learning to Teach Drama 11–18* London: Continuum.

Kempe, A. and Warner, L. (1997) *Starting With Scripts*. Cheltenham: Stanley Thornes.

Kitson, N. and Spiby, I. (1997) *Primary Drama Handbook*. London: Watts Books.

Lacey, S. and Woolland, B. (1989) 'Drama in Education – A Radical Theatre Form', *2D*, Summer, 8(2), 4–15.

Langer, S. (1953) *Feeling and Form*. London: Routledge and Kegan Paul.

Linnell, R. (1988) *Practical Drama Handbook*. London: Hodder & Stoughton.

Linnell, R. (1991) *Theatre Arts Workbook*. London: Hodder & Stoughton.

Lyas, C. (1997) *Aesthetics*. London: UCL Press.

McCleod, J. (1989) 'Drama and Theatre – What's the Fuss?', *Drama Broadsheet*, Autumn, 6(3), 2–6.

McGregor, L., Tate, M. and Robinson, K. (1977) *Learning Through Drama*. London: Heinemann.

McGuire, B. (1998) *Student Handbook for Drama*. Cambridge: Pearson Publishing.

Mackay, S. (1992) 'Not the Drama Quarrel', *2D*, Summer, 11(2), 31–3.

Male, D. (1973) *Approaches to Drama*. London: Unwin.

Marson, P., Brockbank, K., McGuire, B. and Morton, S. (1990) *Drama 14–16*. Cheltenham: Stanley Thornes.

Midgley, M. (1979) *Beast and Man – the Roots of Human Nature*. London: Harvester Press. Reprinted in 1980 by Methuen.

Mitter, S. (1992) *Systems of Rehearsal*. London: Routledge.

Morgan, N. and Saxton, J. (1987) *Teaching Drama*. London: Hutchinson.

Morgan, N. and Saxton, J. (1991) *Teaching, Questioning and Learning*. London: Routledge.

Mukarovsky, J. (1977) *Structure, Sign and Function* (edited and translated by J. Burbank and P. Steiner). New Haven: Yale University Press.

NCC (1990) *The Arts 5–16: A Curriculum Framework*. London: Oliver and Boyd.

NCC (1993) *Teaching History at Key Stage 3*. York: NCC.

Neelands, J. (1990a) *Structuring Drama Work* (edited by T. Goode). Cambridge University Press.

Neelands, J. (1990b) 'The Taylor Interview' (with T. Goode and J. Neelands), *London Drama*, March, 16–19.

Neelands, J. (1991) 'The Meaning of Drama – Part One', *The Drama Magazine*, November, 6–9.

Neelands, J. (1992) *Learning Through Imagined Experience*. London: Hodder & Stoughton.

Neelands, J. (1998) *Begining Drama 11–14*. London: David Fulton Publishers.

Neelands, J. and Dobson, W. (2000) *Drama and Theatre Studies at AS/A Level*. London: Hodder & Stoughton.

Nicholson, H. (ed.) (2000) *Teaching Drama 11–18*. London: Continuum.

Norman, J. (1999) 'Brain right drama', *Drama: The Journal of National Drama* 6(2), 8–13.

Norris, C. (1982) *Deconstruction Theory and Practice*. London: Methuen. Revised edition published in 1991 by Routledge.

O'Neill, C. (1984) 'Imagined Worlds in Theatre and Drama', *London Drama*, Winter, 6(10), 6–9.

O'Neill, C. (1989) 'Ways of Seeing: audience function in drama and theatre', *2D*, Summer, 8(2), 16–29.

O'Neill, C. (1995) *Drama Worlds*. New Hampshire: Heinemann.

O'Neill, C. and Lambert, A. (1982) *Drama Structures: A Practical Handbook for Teachers*. London: Hutchinson.

O'Neill, C., Lambert, A., Linnell, R. and Warr-Wood, J. (1976) *Drama Guidelines*. London: Heinemann.

Osborne, H. (1968) *Aesthetics and Art Theory: An Historical Introduction*. London: Longman.

O'Toole, J. (1992) *The Process of Drama (Negotiating Art and Meaning)*. London: Routledge.

O'Toole, J. and Haseman, B. (1987) *Dramawise – An Introduction to GCSE Drama*. London: Heinemann.

Owens, A. and Barber, K. (1997) *Dramaworks*. Carlisle: Carel Press.

Pemberton-Billing, R. and Clegg, J. (1965) *Teaching Drama*. London: University of London Press.

Pfister, M. (1988) *The Theory and Analysis of Drama*. Cambridge: Cambridge University Press.

Pitcher, G. (1965) 'Emotion', *Mind*, LXXIV. Reprinted in Dearden, P., Hirst, P. and Peters, R. (eds) (1972) *Reason* (Part 2 of *Education and the Development of Reason*). London: Routledge.

Rawlins, G. and Rich, J. (1985) *Look, Listen and Trust*. London: Macmillan. Reprinted in 1992 by Nelson.

Readman, G. (1993) 'Drama in Schools', *Drama*, Spring, 1(2), 2–4.

Readman G. and Lamont, G. (1994) *Drama – A Handbook for Primary Teachers*. London: BBC Education.

Reynolds, P. (1991) *Practical Approaches to Teaching Shakespeare*. Oxford: Oxford University Press.

Robinson, K. (ed.) (1980) *Exploring Theatre and Education*. London: Heinemann.

Rodenburg, P. (1993) *The Need for Words: Voice and the Text*. London: Methuen Drama.

Rodger, I. (1981) *Evacuees*. London: Longman.

Sardo-Brown, B. (1990) 'Experienced Teachers' Planning Practices: a US Survey', *Journal of Education for Teaching*, 16(1), 57–71.

Scrivens, L. (1994) *Drama in the Primary School*. Cambridge: Pearson.

Secondary Heads Association (SHA) (1998) *Drama Sets You Free!* Leicester: SHA.

Sedgwick, F. (1993) *The Expressive Arts*. London: David Fulton Publishers.

Shiach, D. (1987) *Front Page to Performance*. Cambridge: Cambridge University Press.

Slade, P. (1954) *Child Drama*. London: University of London Press.

Smith, R. (1987) 'Teaching on Stilts: a critique of classroom skills', in Holt, M. (ed.) (1987) *Skills and Vocationalism: The Easy Answer*. Milton Keynes: Open University Press, 43–55.

Sockett, H. (1972) 'Curriculum Aims and Objectives: Taking A Means to an End', *Journal of Philosophy of Education*, 6(1). Revised and reprinted in Peters, R. (ed.) (1973) *The Philosophy of Education*. Oxford: Oxford University Press, 150–60.

Somers, J. (1994) *Drama in the Curriculum*. London: Cassell.

Stanislavski, K. (1926) *An Actor Prepares*. London: Geoffrey Bles.

States, B. (1985) *Great Reckonings in Little Rooms: On the Phenomenology of Theater*. California: University of California Press.

Szondi, P. (1987) *Theory of the Modern Drama* (edited and translated by M. Hays). Cambridge: Polity Press.

Tambling, P. (1990) *Performing Arts in the Primary School*. Oxford: Basil Blackwell.

Taylor, C. (1980) 'Thoeries of Meaning', *Proceedings of the British Academy*. Oxford: Oxford University Press, 283–327.

Taylor, C. (1985) *Human Agency and Language – Philosophical Papers 1*. Cambridge: Cambridge University Press.

Taylor, K. (ed.) (1991) *Drama Strategies*. London: Heinemann.

Taylor, P. (ed.) (1996) *Researching Drama and Arts Education*. London: Falmer Press.

Taylor, P. (2000) *The Drama Classroom: Action, Reflection, Transformation*. London: Routledge/Falmer.

Theodoru, M. (1989) *Ideas that Work in Drama*. Cheltenham: Stanley Thornes.

Toye, N. and Prendiville, F. (2000) *Drama and Traditional Story for the Early Years*. London: Routledge.

Veltrusky, J. (1964) 'Man and Object in the Theater', in Garvin, P. (ed.) *A Prague School Reader on Esthetics, Literary Structure and Style*. Washington, D.C.: Georgetown University Press.

Vick, H. (1991) *Applying Drama Methods to the National Curriculum in the Primary School*. Reading: Berkshire Drama and Dance Centre.

Wagner, B. J. (1976) *Dorothy Heathcote: Drama as a Learning Medium*. Washington, D.C.: National Education Association.

Walder, D. (ed.) (1990) *Literature in the Modern World*. Oxford: Oxford University Press in association with the Open University Press.

Wall, G. (1993) 'Resources Pull-Out', *Drama*, Spring, 1(2), 5–8.

Wallis, M. and Shepherd, S. (1998) *Studying Plays*. London: Arnold.

Warburton, N. (1992) *Philosophy – the basics*. London: Routledge.

Watkins, B. (1981) *Drama and Education*. London: Batsford.

Watts, S. and Lee, R. (1991) 'A Monster in the Sea of Humanity', *2D*, Summer, 10(2), 9–15.

Way, B. (1967) *Development Through Drama*. London: Longman.

Williams, S. (1984) 'The Language of Improvised Drama', *Drama Broadsheet*, Summer, 2(3), 9–14.

Winston, J. (1991) 'Planning for Drama in the National Curriculum', *2D*, Winter, 11(1), 7.

Winston, J. (2000) *Drama, Literacy and Moral Education 5–11*. London: David Fulton Publishers.

Winston, J. and Tandy, M. (2001) *Beginning Drama 4–11*. London: David Fulton Publishers. First edition published in 1998.

Wittgenstein, L. (1953) *Philosophical Investigations*. (translated by G.E.M. Anscombe). Oxford: Basil Blackwell.

Woolland, B. (1990) 'Collaborative Teaching in Drama', *London Drama*, July, 4–5.

Woolland, B. (1993) *The Teaching of Drama in the Primary School*. London: Longman.

Wootton, M. (ed.) (1982) *New Directions in Drama Teaching*. London: Heinemann.

Wrack, H. (1992) 'What and How do GCSE Students Learn About the Art Form', *2D*, Summer, 11(2), 14–19.

Index